THE DELICIOUS WAY
TO HELP PROTECT
YOUR HEALTH

Coating the wheat kernel is a substance that can spell the difference between health and illness. That substance is bran, the "forgotten nutrient," so-called because modern food processing has all but destroyed it in the food we eat.

Now doctors say that this unique food may help save your life. This book presents the medical facts and gives you doctor-suggested programs that may help you protect your body against cancer, restore the basic health of your bowels and intestines, and shield you from a variety of circulatory and heart diseases such as varicose veins, "hardening" of the arteries, and more.

You'll also find dozens of delicious ways to use this life-saving discovery in meat, fish and poultry main dishes, soups and salads, breads and rolls, desserts and snacks, beverages and other ways.

Rediscover bran—and add vitality to your life!

THE BOOK OF BRAN

CARLSON WADE

A JOVE / HBJ BOOK

Two Pyramid printings
First Jove/HBJ edition published October 1977

Library of Congress Catalog Card Number: 76-14623

Printed in the United States of America

Jove/HBJ books are published by Jove Publications, Inc. (Harcourt Brace Jovanovich), 757 Third Avenue, New York, N.Y. 10017

CONTENTS

6   CONTENTS

INTRODUCTION

On the outside of the wheat kernel is a substance that can spell the difference between health and illness—and life, itself. Called *bran*, it is the tough, chewy outer coating of the unrefined wheat kernel. It is also known as *roughage* or *cellulose*, or more popularly as *fiber*. It is considered a "forgotten nutrient" because modern refining and food processing as well as chemical adulteration have all but destroyed its presence in food. Because of its decline in food, there has been a medically reported decline in health.

But new medical research has revived interest in bran. Doctors now say that the life of the kernel of wheat can also be the life of the human body. Bran is more than a chewy food. It is a form of bulk that is able to help protect the body against cancer. It also helps restore the basic health of the bowels and intestines. Bran is also found to be the most healthful to the heart and the circulatory systems. Bran is also an important and little-known nutrient that is able to control cholesterol, the suspected element in heart trouble.

Medical men report that in those countries or civilizations where bran is eaten daily, there is a natural immunity to the life-devouring ailments such as cancer and heart trouble.

In the underdeveloped countries, where food is not tampered with, where there is no refining, those people enjoy a whole-grain and high-fiber diet and are remarkably immune from the well-known diseases of the more developed countries. This vital ingredient, bran, appears to be the miracle substance that has long been sought as a natural way to fortify the body against the ravages of ill health. A high-fiber diet, with emphasis on bran, is con-

7

sidered to be a powerful bulwark against the most serious diseases of Western civilization.

This book will show you how medical research proves the effectiveness of bran in helping to shield and insulate the body against diseases. It will tell you what bran does for your body, where to find bran, how to use bran.

This book will also give you descriptive lists of major fiber-creating foods in addition to bran, so that you can enjoy this life-saving food in endless dishes, easily prepared.

If there is to be one miracle diet discovery of the century, it may well be bran. It is the most exciting discovery in our modern times. And it is much, much more, as this book will show you. Enter a world that offers hope for everlasting health—with bran.

—CARLSON WADE

Part I

BRAN AND FIBER
IN YOUR LIFE

CHAPTER 1

BRAN—WHAT IT IS AND
WHAT IT CAN DO FOR YOU

A little-known, newly discovered substance in food is being hailed as an important protective element against many common and uncommon digestive ailments. That substance is known as *fiber*, an ingredient found in plant foods, but especially abundant in a rediscovered food, namely *bran*. This grain food, a prime source of fiber, is considered an important all-natural protective shield against ailments afflicting the tissue cells, in cholesterol control, and against the risk of cancer, bowel-intestinal ailments, heart distress, and many other ravages of modern civilization.

What is bran and what can it do to protect your health? Let us begin with some of the basics about this important food.

BRAN. Bran is the outermost layer of the grain seed or kernel. It is the tough, chewy outer coating of the unrefined wheat kernel. This part of the seed also contains a major share of the nutrients in grain, including many vitamins and minerals. A bran cereal has been prepared by having the cleaned bran ground and passed through grooved rollers to produce the characteristic shred of this grain. Basically, bran is the broken coat of the seed of the cereal grain separated from the flour or meal by sifting or bolting (a machine process which sifts the wheat kernel or grain seed through fine-meshed cloth).

CELLULOSE. A form of bulk, created by bran, that swells up so that it can pass through the intestines and maintain regularity, or protect against constipation.

FIBER. Also called roughage, fiber is found in the cell walls of all plant foods to some extent, but in varying amounts and types. *Bran is considered to be one of the best sources of fiber.* It is that portion of the plant cell wall that largely resists digestion. Plant cell walls are complex structures that contain a number of different types of polysaccharides (carbohydrates that can be decomposed by hydrolysis or liquid action), including pectin, hemicelluloses, celluloses, and lignin. Traces of protein, complex lipids, and variable amounts of inorganic matter are also found in the cell walls. Fiber most often appears to be equated with the largely indigestible cellulose and lignin components of that plant cell wall.

ROUGHAGE. Another name for fiber, roughage is bulk. That is, roughage is coarse bulky food (bran is the best source of roughage) that is relatively high in fiber and low in digestible nutrients. By its bulk, it stimulates peristalsis, successive waves of involuntary contraction passing along the walls of the intestine to create a bowel movement. Roughage, or fiber, as found in bran, is needed to create regularity to maintain good health.

HOW BRAN-CREATED FIBER CREATES GOOD HEALTH

Basically, bran-created fiber is an insoluble substance that forms the strengthening tissue of plants. It is not digested because it is not affected by the acids or alkalies of digestive processes but passes through the alimentary tract with little change. In so doing, bran-created fiber sweeps the intestinal tract clean. *The key to its health building properties lies in the rate of passage time of ingested food. Fiber increases this rate. This is most important to your health.*

It was Denis Burkitt, M.D., and coresearcher, Dr. Neil Painter, who, first reporting in May 22, 1971, to the *British Medical Journal,* noted that certain diseases of the large bowel were rare among the rural people of underdeveloped countries where the diet is high in fiber-containing foods. They theorized that a lack of sufficient fiber played a role in the development of certain health problems of Western countries and the rate at which the problems have appeared. Doctors Burkitt and Painter suggested that a faster fiber-passage rate has a beneficial effect upon basic health. *Eating more bran foods will create more fiber and apparently hasten the passing of this bulk and create a natural barrier against many so-called "diseases of civilization."*

Doctors Burkitt and Painter reported that people in more primitive countries eat high-residue diets (high fiber) and their food passes through more quickly.

People in developed Western countries eat low-residue diets (low fiber) because of refining and processing, and their food passes through very slowly, sometimes taking as long as four to six days.

Basic Problem of A Low-Fiber Diet. A low bran-created fiber diet means a slower passage of food. This allows bacteria in the intestines to combine with food particles (often high in chemical preservatives) and create carcinogenic (cancer-causing) substances. The problem is that the slow-moving food mass containing chemical additives may infect cells and tissues of the intestinal and digestive regions and create a condition favorable for cancer of the colon, diverticulosis, hemorrhoids, ulcerated colitis, and related ailments.

Food should pass through quickly or it becomes lodged in small pockets of the intestinal canal. These pockets are called diverticula. Excessive amounts of lodged food may cause *diverticulosis* or inflammation of this region, a forerunner of cancer in complicated situations. To hasten passage of food, the diet needs to be high in fiber, which is found in bran.

Refined Foods Are Deficient in Fiber. When the milling of our grains began in 1880, the valuable fiber (along with vitamins and minerals) was removed from many foods. Bran, *when processed,* may also be deficient in this fiber. It was shortly after this refining process began that many ailments of the digestive system began to appear. A deficiency in fiber is believed to be the cause of many of these digestive-intestinal ailments. Drs. Burkitt and Painter reported that diverticular disease of the colon is very prevalent in countries deficient in fiber. The doctors cured this problem by adding *unprocessed bran* to the diets of the patients. The doctors affirm that unprocessed grain foods, particularly bran, are needed as a healthy and all-natural way to protect against digestive-intestinal illnesses and to hasten the passage time of wastes and protect against other ailments, including cancer of the bowel.

Helps Control Weight. Fiber-containing bran, as well as fibrous foods such as raw fruits and vegetables and unprocessed grains, gives you a feeling of fullness. It creates natural bulk. This helps control your appetite, and you can actually lose weight since you will have less desire to eat high-calorie foods.

Controls Cholesterol. Fiber-containing bran, reports Dr. David Kritchevsky of the Wistar Institute of Philadelphia, works in the intestinal tract to "bind" bile salts, which are produced from cholesterol. The bound bile salts are then excreted by the body. In a sense, it is as if the bran "arrested" the bile salts and led them away. The body then makes more bile salts from stored reserves of cholesterol. The net result is a significant lowering of cholesterol in the blood.

WHY ALL-NATURAL BRAN IS THE KEY TO BETTER HEALTH

Refined or processed bran foods are considered inadequate since the fiber content has been altered or destroyed and cannot efficiently hasten the cleansing action in the intestines.

R. Swinburne Clymer, M.D., writing in *Diet: A Key To Health*, explains that when bran is processed, the protein and nuclein contents are separated and "violence is done, and a natural food [bran], created *balanced* by Nature, is thereby destructive."

Dr. Clymer notes that a refined product "torn from its originally accompanying elements and taken out of its natural combination, produces a nascent lactic acid both in mouth and stomach. This acid, taken up by the system, is destructive to health." Dr. Clymer says that only all-natural bran is the key to better health.

Furthermore, Dr. Clymer says that all-natural and non-processed bran is "recommended because it is partially digested, because it is rich in the organic mineral elements which the organs of assimilation do extract or absorb despite its incomplete digestion—elements which are positively essential in maintaining the equilibrium of the tissues and in rebuilding tissue.

"The bran, not being wholly digested, acts as an eliminator, scouring the mucous of intestines and bowels, and thus helps to produce natural peristaltic action."

You may ask, if bran is not completely digested how can its mineral and other elements be assimilated by the system? The answer is found in the *method* used by the digestive and assimilative organs. Namely, they secrete a solvent or an enzyme that "tears apart" eaten bran, and extracts its fiber, which is then passed through "the digestive and eliminative organism in a more or less whole state and thus cleanses and eliminates the poisons and toxins from the bowels," says Dr. Clymer.

Summing up, Dr. Clymer relates, "The greater portion of bran ingested is not digested but it is *mascerated* in the digestive juices. Now a mascerated mass of any substance need not be 'digested' in order that its virtues or active principles be extracted, but the solvent employed (digestive enzyme) if of the right kind, will extract it.

"So with the assimilation of the real constructive particles in bran. The digestive juices act as the solvent and absorb, or 'draw out' these qualities even though the bran is not actually digested."

Therefore, bran may be partially digested, but its beneficial nutrients are removed through the enzymatic processes and believed to create healing benefits. The emphasis is on all-natural or whole-grain bran, which is a prime source of the fiber needed to sweep clean the intestinal tract. Dr. Clymer says that good health is possible with "the combination of protein, vitamins, organic mineral elements and nuclein in the original food substance created by Nature. This combination, besides yielding these various important elements, also prevents the formation of noxious acids and gases which form when denatured white or milled flour is largely consumed as food."

TAKING A LOOK AT (NNF) NON-NUTRITIVE FIBER

Non-nutritive fiber is a component of bran that passes through the entire digestive system without being totally broken down or absorbed. NNF is not a vitamin. It supplies no nutrients. Instead, the foods containing fiber also contain vitamins and minerals and protein, which are healthful for the body.

The Bureau of Nutrition of the New York City Health Department has this to say about a new look at fiber: "During recent years, we've become very concerned about the vitamins, minerals and protein in the foods we eat, but we've paid little attention to their fiber content.

"Now, scientists are taking another look at fiber and its relation to health. Some believe that the shift in our eating habits over the past 50 years from diets high in fiber, particularly in whole-grain bread and cereals, to diets low in fiber may be linked to a broad spectrum of diseases.

"Today, many of us eat more low-fiber foods such as refined bread and cereals. More meat, more processed foods, more sugar and fat than ever before.

"*Some scientists think that low-fiber diets may be associated with diseases of the intestinal tract like diverticulosis, cancer of colon, as well as heart diseases and others.*

"As a prudent preventive measure, many Americans should eat more fiber-rich foods. Your best sources include bran, whole grain breads and cereals, dry beans and peas, nuts, fruits and vegetables. (Fiber or roughage is that part of a plant food which is not digested.) Foods rich in fiber are generally rich in vitamins and minerals and for that reason alone would be highly recommended."

Noted nutritionist Dr. Jean Mayer of Harvard University noted in his syndicated column (September 3, 1975) that fiber is essential to the diet. "I believe that fiber is a highly useful component of a good diet and that we need more of it in the typical American menu.

"Fiber is a catch-all word for several hard substances that support and protect the walls and cells of plants. In our stomachs, fiber is separated from digestible substances and it passes through the intestines more or less unchanged.

"But it is in this passage through the intestines that fiber exerts its most beneficial effect for humans. In our diet, the main sources of roughage are the outer husks of any grain (usually wheat bran) and the fibers from vegetables such as cooked spinach or raw carrots. Roughage adds bulk to the stool, making it larger, and absorbs moisture, making it softer.

"We do know enough about the relationship between a high-fiber diet and intestinal health to say that adding more fiber to the typical American diet is a good thing."

GETTING ACQUAINTED WITH BRAN

Bran may be tough, but it's chewy good. It gives a lot of healthful exercise to your teeth and gums. It alerts your digestive system to secrete more enzymes to better improve metabolism. It's deliciously exciting to become better acquainted with bran. Use it in any of these forms:

• Sprinkle bran over your favorite whole-grain cereal.

• Make a cereal of bran, chopped nuts and seeds, sun-dried fruits, and skim milk.

• Mix one-half cup of granola cereal with one-half cup of bran. Add skim milk. Let soak a few minutes before eating.

• Add bran to any prepared food such as soups, casseroles, meat or fish loaves. Use it as a sprinkling on top of fruit or vegetable salads.

• When doing any baking, just leave out a little of the flour and replace with bran.

NUTRITIVE POWER IN BRAN
(About 3½ ounces, or ½ cup, or 100 grams)

Protein—12.6 grams
Phosphorus—1,176 milligrams
Iron—8.8 milligrams
Thiamine—0.10 milligrams
Riboflavin—0.29 milligrams
Niacin—17.8 milligrams

CHAPTER 2

BRAN: DOCTORS' HOPE FOR
NATURAL CANCER CONTROL

In the United States cancer of the colon is a cause of death second only to lung cancer. It strikes nearly 75,000 men and women a year. It kills 46,000 a year. Cancer of the colon strikes most frequently those populations which also have a high rate of diverticular disease. It led many medical researchers to find a cause of cancer and a possible form of natural control. One physician, Denis Burkitt, M.D., reported that a low-fiber diet could predispose the body to formation of cancer. As a hope for natural cancer control, the doctor said the diet should be high in fiber such as bran.

How Waste Irritation Is a Possible Cancer Cause. Speaking before the 1971 meeting of the National Conference on Cancer of the Colon and Rectum in San Diego, California, Dr. Burkitt said that waste (fecal) matter contains several known carcinogenic (cancer-causing) substances. These substances may be present in a normal diet in small amounts, or may be produced in the intestinal tract as body bacteria acts upon waste matter.

Dr. Burkitt pointed out that in developed countries where refined "mushy" foods are eaten, the waste matter is in contact with the membranous lining of the intestines about two and one half times as long as it is with the intestinal lining of people in underdeveloped countries. Therefore, there is much more opportunity for these potential carcinogens to irritate the lining. Again, the amount of time that waste remains in the system appears to be a causative factor in cancer. The slower the waste is removed, the greater the risk of cancer. The quicker the waste is removed, the less chance there is of a cancer risk.

Dr. Burkitt also explained that the primitive person who has a high-fiber diet with nonprocessed foods and whole-grain bran, will have a stool that is about four times as large as a Westerner. The reason is that people in underdeveloped countries eat more fiber-containing bran; together with liquids, any carcinogens in the stool will be much less concentrated than they are in the small hard stool of Westerners. Dr. Burkitt also noted that storage time is longest near the end of the bowel.

(The *Journal of the AMA*, in its February 1, 1971, issue, reported that 44.3 per cent of colonic cancers arise within the last six inches of the gastrointestinal tract.)

Refined Foods Are Possible Cancer Risks. Dr. Burkitt expressed concern over the large amounts of refined carbohydrates eaten by civilized nations; he believed that this could trigger off cancer of the colon. He said, "It is most likely that all of this sugar alters the composition of the intestinal flora; it may also react in different ways with the otherwise harmless substance released by these bacteria" and create a predisposition to cancer of the colon. This need not be so with natural and unrefined foods such as whole-grain bran! Elimination of all refined foods could be a natural way to protect the body against cancer.

Bile Acid Is One Clue. Dr. Burkitt expressed the theory that refined carbohydrates may destroy bile acids somewhere in the intestine, removing a protective substance against cancer. While comparatively little may be known about the complex interactions of substances in the lower end of the digestive tract, it is believed that a refined carbohydrate diet and small stools should alert people to possible ill health in this part of the body.

Dr. Burkitt, speaking to the specialists, said that there were probably many causes of colonic cancer. But he insisted that a diet high in bran fiber and low in refined carbohydrates would be a sensible precaution.

CANCER AND DIET: A DOCTOR'S HIGH-BRAN PROGRAM

A doctor has discovered that a simple high bran program, together with medical supervision, can help provide protection and some degree of natural resistance to cancer of the colon and other body organs.

High-Bran Foods Are Protective. Ian MacGregor, M.D., reporting his findings to the *Journal of the AMA* (February 25, 1974) says that a food program high in fiber-creating bran can prevent many colonic troubles, including that of cancer. (The colon is the lower part of the digestive tract, also known as the large intestine.)

"Evidence suggests," says Dr. MacGregor, "that this high incidence of large-bowel cancer, like that of lung cancer, may be a relatively recent development." He says it is "rare in underdeveloped countries" where the diet is high in whole grains, bran, and *unrefined* foods. Dr. MacGregor explains that eating much fiber-creating bran can offer a natural protection against forms of colonic cancer.

Refined Foods Are Unhealthy. "The unabsorbable fiber content of food is discarded in the milling and preparation of the refined foods of our Western diet," says the doctor. "We consider this unabsorbable fiber content one of the most notable differences between the diet of the Western world, where cancer is prevalent, and the diet of the underdeveloped countries, where the incidence of cancer is low."

Dr. MacGregor says that refined foods are unhealthy, void of fiber, and may predispose to cancer of the colon.

Intestinal Bacteria May Be Cancer Cause. Dr. MacGregor observes that a type of bacteria that inhabit the intestinal tract (especially the colon) can convert certain ingredients into cancer-causing substances. But a high-fiber-creating bran diet keeps such bacteria under control and can even eliminate these harmful organisms, thereby reducing the risk of cancer.

Protective Action of Bran. As a high-fiber food, bran helps create bulky stools, which says Dr. MacGregor, move along much more quickly, so that if any cancer-causing substances are present, they have a reduced time in which to be in contact with the walls of the intestines.

The doctor explains that a deficiency of fiber leads to smaller, less bulky stools, which hold the risky substance in more highly concentrated form and create a greater cancer-causing threat to the colon.

Fat + Sugar = Cancer Risk. Colonic Bacteria becomes altered because of a very high fat and/or sugar diet, says Dr. MacGregor. Specifically, he refers to processed and refined foods. The doctor feels that if the food program eliminated excess fat and refined foods, the colonic cancer would be less disturbed and there would be more protection against the risk of cancer.

Fiber Also Helps Control Cholesterol. As an added bonus for eating fiber-building foods such as bran, Dr. MacGregor says the levels of cholesterol could be controlled, as noted in tests on selected patients. The blood cholesterol levels decreased from 206 milligrams to 160 milligrams almost immediately. While bran is of invaluable help, chick peas (garbanzo beans), and alfalfa were also helpful. (Alfalfa contains a substance called *saponin* that joins with excess cholesterol and then helps wash it out of the body.)

Fiber-Containing Foods. To help keep your colon, along with the rest of your body, in good health and to protect yourself against cancer and other ailments, your daily food program should include bran as the forerunner of high-fiber foods. Others include whole-grain breads and cereals, natural brown rice, wheat germ, all nuts and seeds, sun-dried fruits, fibrous vegetables, sunflower seeds. TIP: Add seeds and nuts when making meat loaves or hamburger patties. Use seeds and nuts as snacks, with fruits as desserts.

SAMPLE MENU

Here's a typical day's menu of high-fiber-creating bran foods:

BREAKFAST:
Fruit juice
Two eggs
Whole grain toast
Bran cereal with milk

LUNCHEON:
Chopped chicken on whole-grain bread
Tossed raw vegetable salad with seeds, nuts
Fresh fruit slices
Seasonal fruit compote with chopped nuts

DINNER:
Broiled or baked meat
Brown rice with chopped seeds, nuts
Steamed vegetable (broccoli, squash, etc.)
Fresh fruit slices
Assorted seeds and nuts

Summing Up: Dr. MacGregor believes that colonic cancer could be dramatically reduced with a doctor-supervised program that emphasizes high-fiber bran and other foods in the diet. He believes that this program also offers protection against and healing of related disorders such as constipation, diverticulitis, colitis, diarrhea. It's believed to be the natural way to guard your body against cancer!

A LOW-MEAT, HIGH-FIBER DIET PROTECTS AGAINST CANCER

A simple dietary change in which the meat intake is reduced and the high-fiber bran intake is increased, can offer good protection against cancer. In particular, meat reduction is most helpful in building body resistance to cancer. Epidemiologists (research specialists in studying illnesses that affect a large percentage of the population) report that in countries where there is a low meat intake, cancer is markedly reduced.

A study prepared for the Pan American Health Organization shows that in countries such as England or Argentina, as well as the United States, where meat consumption is high, there is a correspondingly higher colonic cancer rate. But in countries such as Guatemala and Colombia, where meat consumption is low and fiber intake is high, there is a much lower rate of colonic cancer.

Furthermore, in the more developed Western nations where beef intake is high, there is also a high consumption of saturated fat, sugar, white flour, and other animal protein and a markedly low intake of natural fiber and roughage. The link between high meat intake and cancer appeared evident according to this study.

Beef Consumption "Encourages" Colonic Cancer. "There is now substantial evidence that beef consumption is a key factor in determining bowel-cancer incidence," said John W. Berg, M.D., before the second National Conference on Cancer of the Colon and Rectum, held in Florida in 1973. Together with his coworker, Margaret A. Howell, Ph.D., he told how two very high beef-eating nations (which also have low fiber intake) have correspondingly high rates of cancer.

Doctors Berg and Howell reported that Scotland has "reclaimed her usual distinction of having the world's highest death rate from bowel cancer." These very high rates are found in the beef-raising areas around Aberdeen. "The Scots eat 19 per cent more beef than the English and have a 19 per cent higher mortality rate from bowel cancer."

The doctors then told of having done research among Japanese who emigrated to Hawaii, or those who were the children of Japanese of previous generations who settled in the islands. These peoples gave up their Japanese-style diet and succumbed to a high-meat Western diet and the result is that they had a very high incidence of colonic cancer.

Reporting to the *Journal of the National Cancer Institute* (December, 1973) Doctors Berg and Howell tell us, "The bowel cancer risks for both Issei (immigrants) and Nisei (children of immigrants), who at the time of interview had discontinued the daily practice of taking one or more Japanese-style meals (low beef and high fiber), were roughly double those for individuals persisting in this practice—a significant and numerically important difference."

This suggests that when meat intake is very high, at the sacrifice of fiber, there is a greater risk and occurrence of bowel cancer.

The researchers note, "Meat provides a striking example of a change in food practices between Japan and Hawaii—the rise in beef consumption—to parallel the upward displacement of bowel cancer risk among Japanese migrants."

AMERICAN MEAT CONSUMPTION
POSES CANCER RISK

Dr. Berg and his researchers further report that in areas of America where meat consumption is higher, there is a correspondingly higher cancer rate.

They note that in the South and in those populations where more poultry and fiber-creating grains are eaten, there is less incidence of colon in cancer. But people who live in the cities and eat high amounts of beef have a higher incidence of colonic cancer.

Fat Displaces Roughage. High fat intake appears to displace roughage as a substance in the body. Yet fat does not have the "cleansing" power of bran and is of little help in offering protection against cancer. On the contrary, it presents a risk to the health of the colon.

The researchers tell us, "Beef coming to urban markets

from feeding lots has a substantial fat content. While the same comment would now hold true for beef supplied to rural populations through normal commercial channels, much of the beef used by farm populations in the past must have come from local slaughter of young cattle with a low fat content closely resembling that in veal. *We have found . . . no populations with a high beef intake and a low rate of bowel cancer."*

Summing up, the researchers point out that Seventh Day Adventists, most of whom are vegetarians, show 20 per cent less of a death rate from intestinal cancer.

This discovery was reported in *Lancet* (January 16, 1971, p. 98) some years before when doctors noted, "People living in the areas with a high recorded incidence of carcinoma (cancer) of the colon tend to live on diets containing large amounts of fat and animal protein, whereas those who live in areas with a low incidence live on largely vegetarian diets [which are also high in bran] with little fat or animal matter."

American Meat Eating Traced to Cancer Increase. More proof of the cancer risk involved in heavy meat eating is offered by Dr. Margaret Howell, in the *Journal of Chronic Diseases* (1975, Vol. 28, pp. 67–80). Dr. Howell refers to Department of Agriculture studies of certain cities: Buffalo, Minneapolis–St. Paul, San Francisco, and Birmingham in which meat eating was very high. Dr. Howell says that death rates caused by colonic cancer for these four cities is correspondingly higher than those of cities where meat consumption is lower.

Dr. Howell concludes: *"Beef or cattle meat is probably the most suspect of the meats (as a cancer cause) . . . The evidence suggests that meat, particularly beef, is a food associated with the development of malignancies of the large bowel."*

How Beef May Trigger Risk of Intestinal Cancer. Dr. M. J. Hill of the Bacterial Metabolism Research Laboratory of London's Central Public Health Laboratory, reporting in *Lancet* (March 8, 1975) says that the high-fat, high-beef Western diet influences the lower digestive tract in these two ways:

1. The level of waste bile acids and neutral steroids is raised to an unhealthy level.

2. Two of these substances, *deoxycholic acid* and *lithocholic acid,* are known to be cocarcinogenic in test animals. They are particularly cancer causing in the rectum.

Dr. Hill also says that a high animal fat diet increases an unhealthy bacterial count. A particular bacteria, *Clostridium paraputrificum,* concentrated in the intestine, has the ability to convert certain bile acids into risky carcinogens.

Dr. Hill reports that the levels of waste bile acids and *clostridia* are much higher in the wastes of those persons who subsist on a high meat diet and also show a higher incidence of colonic cancer. Newly diagnosed bowel-cancer patients were said to have the highest levels of all of these unhealthy waste bile acids and bacteria.

A DIET CHANGE CAN OFFER PROTECTION AGAINST CANCER

Dr. M. J. Hill, reporting also to the *American Journal of Clinical Nutrition* (December, 1974) says that a diet change can offer protection against the risk of cancer. "Colon cancer can be prevented by modifying the diet."

Dr. Hill says that vegans (those who eat no meat or any source of animal protein such as eggs, cheese, milk) have one-half the waste bile acid concentrations of their meat-eating counterparts. This type of meatless or vegan diet may be difficult for many people.

Dr. Hill recognizes it and offers a compromise: "a mere halving of the daily fat intake to 50–60 grams per day would result in a much reduced fecal [waste] bile acid concentration while still leaving a very acceptable diet."

Because beef is the food higher in saturated fats than most others, it would be wise to reduce beef intake by one-half.

AN EASY 5-STEP PLAN TO LOW-MEAT, HIGH-FIBER INTAKE

Physicians at the School of Health of Loma Linda University, Loma Linda, California, have prepared this easy 5-step plan that reduces meat intake, increases fiber intake, and adds up to good taste and food enjoyment, while building better health and resistance to cancer:

1. Cut "empty calories" by at least half. About 35 per cent of calories in the typical American diet are from sugars and fats. Another 20 per cent from bread and cereals of which more than 90 per cent are refined. Simply by adding these figures you can see that more than one-half of the calories that many Americans eat are from refined and processed foods. Many diets would be greatly improved by switching from empty calories to unrefined foods. (These include whole grains, especially bran.)

2. Replace meat in the protein group. Use a variety of legumes and meat analogs made from wheat, bran, and/or soy proteins to replace the protein, calories, vitamins, and minerals in meat. Many common and excellent combinations can be planned by using whole-grain bran cereals and legumes such as lentil-rice loaf, oat-soy waffles, corn-lima-bean succotash, or garbanzos (chick peas) served with cornbread. The peanut butter and whole wheat sandwich, a favorite of children and many adults, too, is a good combination.

Nuts make a good addition to your meals, contributing protein, a generous amount of unsaturated (desirable kind) fat, and a great deal of satiety (satisfaction). They must be used in moderation; one-fourth cup of shelled nuts is about right for any one meal. Although commercially prepared meat alternates are not essential to a well-balanced vegetarian diet, these convenience foods do help, as every homemaker knows. There are a number of canned, dehydrated, and frozen convenience foods available in health stores and supermarkets today.

Eggs are excellent protein sources, too, and provide vitamin B_{12} for the diet. Because they contain large amounts of cholesterol, two or three a week are plenty.

3. Increase the use of low-fat milk products. As you increase the use of nonfat or low-fat milk products such as cottage cheese, you add protein and other nutrients, especially calcium, riboflavin (a B vitamin), and vitamin B_{12} 'o the diet.

4. Increase the use of foods from the bran cereal and bread group. Since this group supplies protein to your diet, as well as iron and B vitamins, your use of breads and bran cereals—preferably in the whole-grain form—should be somewhat increased. However, you should be careful that this increase does not take place at the expense of other food groups.

5. Use plenty of fruits and vegetables. Although this group gives us less than 10 per cent of our calories, fruits and vegetables supply almost all of the vitamin C and about one-half of the vitamin A values along with substantial amounts of other nutrients. Fruits and vegetables deserve a prominent place in any good diet.

HOW EXTRA FIBER IN THE FORM OF BRAN PROTECTS AGAINST CANCER OF THE COLON

Extra dietary fiber in the form of bran offers a natural form of protection against the risk of colonic cancer. This is the finding made by doctors E. W. Pomare and K. W. Heaton of the British Royal Infirmary as reported to the *British Medical Journal* (November 3, 1973).

Doctors Pomare and Heaton say that about 33 grams of bran (about 5 tablespoonsful) eaten daily helps to create important cancer-protective changes in bile salt metabolism. It is suggested that this amount of bran should be from an unprocessed or natural source; it can be taken with beverages, mixed into cereals, casseroles, soups, stews or in bread for more palatability.

THE MAGIC CANCER-FIGHTING ACTION OF BRAN FIBER

To begin, let's take a closer look at bran fiber so we can better understand how it has a magic cancer-fighting action.

What Is Bran Fiber? It is the indigestible, structural part of the outer layers of the wheat kernel. It is composed of complex carbohydrates including cellulose, hemi-cellulose, pectin, and lignin, which is a woody substance.

What Does It Do? Basically, bran fiber provides bulk that absorbs moisture and helps your digestive system keep clean and self-regulate its activities.

Why Is It Important? It appears to hasten the removal of waste matter and thereby protect the intestinal canal from putrefactive bacteria that may predispose it to cancer. Furthermore, a high-bran-fiber program makes you less prone to general digestive problems.

Bran fiber offers a unique cancer protective action in these three forms:

1. Bran fiber acts directly on the intestinal microflora, either inhibiting or removing the production of cancer-causing agents.

2. Bran fiber hastens the transit time of waste and this reduces the time allowed for carcinogens in the wastes to interact with the wall of the bowel. Dr. Denis Burkitt says in *Lancet* (December 30, 1972) that waste matter remains in contact with the intestinal lining of the Westerner more than twice as long as with the intestinal lining of someone from an underdeveloped country who eats a natural, high-

fiber diet. The Westerner also has a correspondingly higher intestinal cancer rate.

3. Bran fiber increases the moisture content and bulk of the stool. This dilutes the concentration of potential cancer-causing substances. Bran fiber thus blocks their contact with the intestinal wall, creating a "shield" or "insulation" that reduces risk of colon cancer.

Bran Fiber And Gallstones. An added bonus of bran fiber (in addition to its reported ability to block chemical changes associated with bowel cancer) is that it is believed to help protect or treat gallstones. Dr. E. W. Pomare, writing in *Internal Medicine News* (March 1, 1975), says that at the British Royal Infirmary, *when gallstone patients were fed as much bran daily as they could take, the cholesterol saturation of the bile was significantly lowered.*

Dr. Pomare recommends using completely unprocessed bran such as found in health food stores. He also said that the larger particle size of unprocessed bran is more effective than the smaller particles found in packaged dry cereals. Furthermore, he feels that regular intake of bran could help reduce the size of existing gallstones.

THE DANGEROUS CANCER AGENT
FOUND IN BEEF

A potent carcinogen has been identified in beef. Called *malonaldehyde,* it was identified by Raymond J. Shamberger, Ph.D., a scientist with the biochemistry department of the Cleveland Clinic Foundation.

Dr. Shamberger told the 1975 meeting of the American Association for Cancer Research in San Diego, California, that *malonaldehyde* is an extremely reactive breakdown product that begins to form in flesh almost immediately after the animal is slaughtered. Dr. Shamberger applied *malonaldehyde* to test animals. Within three weeks after the experiment was finished, 52 per cent of the animals had developed tumors.

Writing in the *Journal of the National Cancer Institute* (December, 1974), Dr. Shamberger says that *"malonaldehyde* might be the ultimate carcinogen."

Risk Is Present for Humans. Dr. Shamberger says, "We can suspect a similar effect on the human digestive tract when *malonaldehyde* is carried to it in foods. The substance could act alone in humans or it may act in conjunction with substances such as bile acids, which are known tumor promoters.

"We know that the entire human digestive system is exposed to *malonaldehyde* because we find it in feces. In addition, we know that the incidence of many types of human cancer increases with age. This raises the question of whether or not human stomach, colon, and other digestive tract cancers are due to a dose-response effect; that is, an accumulation of *malonaldehyde*'s actions in the body. Our calculations indicate that a typical American diet contains much more *malonaldehyde* during a lifetime than we gave the test animals."

Dosages That Are Lethal. "If we could use just simple comparative calculations we could say that a person of average height and weight would have to consume about 15 grams of *malonaldehyde* to get an amount equal to the lowest dose that produced cancer in test animals . . . We estimate the typical American diet contains about 1.1 grams per year or roughly 75 grams in a lifetime—comparatively far more than the test animals received.

"It is not that simple, though, since we know that only 1 per cent of the substance that we applied to the test animals was effective— 99 per cent was destroyed by the air. The amounts in the human gastrointestinal tract should not be destroyed by air and should be 100 per cent effective and therefore almost 99 times as potent as the test animal doses.

"So for example, by the time a person is 30 he would have consumed twice the dose we gave the test animals and it may be 100 times more potent, equaling a dose of 200 times that given the mice. In a lifetime then, the dose would be five times the mouse dose, totally 500 times the potency."

Less Beef—More Bran. Judging the cancer risk found in beef, it would appear to be prudent to use less beef. It is also advisable to substitute bran as a means of taking in plant protein as well as vitamin and minerals and also fiber, which is used for scrubbing the intestinal regions. It is a simple program. It can save your life!

IF YOU MUST EAT BEEF

Dr. Raymond J. Shamberger offers these suggestions for those who must eat beef, but want to reduce the risk of *malonaldehyde* accumulation in the body:

1. Thaw frozen meat in the refrigerator with the wrapper intact. Do not leave it out to thaw at room temperature. It is believed this inhibits the formation of *malonaldehyde.*

2. After eating a meat meal, if you have leftovers, immediately wrap and cover them and place in your refrigerator.

3. Note that *malonaldehyde* is also formed during decomposition of polyunsaturated oils. Therefore, Dr. Shamberger suggests that those on a high polyunsaturated program take daily supplements of vitamin C and vitamin E. These nutrients are natural antioxidants. They help halt the breakdown of polyunsaturated fats into *malonaldehyde.*

4. If you must eat beef cut down on the amounts you consume. This includes other meats, too. Moderation is the watchword.

"I have reduced my own meat consumption by almost 50 per cent," says Dr. Shamberger. "Life is a series of risks. As individuals and as a society we can and should identify the risks and reduce or eliminate as many as possible. If we have adequate information we can knowingly choose those we wish to encounter or avoid. That process of selection is a very personal matter."

Since beef is identified as a cancer-causing risk, then reduction or elimination can very well be a decision that will lengthen your health span and lifetime!

As a life-saving food, bran should be part of your daily diet . . . for the rest of your long life!

CHAPTER 3

HOW BRAN HELPS REBUILD YOUR BOWELS AND INTESTINES

A simple food element is reported to be a natural way to help rebuild your bowels and intestines. The element is *bran,* the coat of the seed of whole-wheat grain. It is said to be one of the most effective (and totally natural) remedies for many ailments of the digestive-eliminative systems.

BRAN CORRECTS "IRRITABLE BOWEL SYNDROME"

Patients troubled with so-called "irritable bowel syndrome" were treated with bran, which helped correct disorders. Lieutenant Joseph L. Piepmeyer, M.D., in the Medical Service Corps of the U.S. Naval Reserve, stationed at Beaufort Naval Hospital in South Carolina, reported to the *American Journal of Clinical Nutrition* (Vol. 27, February, 1974) that he treated some thirty out-patients troubled with "irritable bowel syndrome" with bran.

Dr. Piepmeyer says his patients had abnormal bowel habits, a vicious cycle of constipation followed by the passage of difficult wastes, followed in turn by diarrhea. Dr. Piepmeyer says many of his patients also had problems of digestive cramps and stomach bloating.

(Other names for this set of problems include irritable colon, adaptive colitis, mucous colitis, spastic colon, and unstable colon.)

Dr. Piepmeyer says that the thirty patients had no organic cause of this set of problems. He put his patients on a simple bran-healing program, as follows:

1. Every day, eat from 8 to 10 rounded teaspoons of unprocessed bran, either alone or with other foods, prepared in any desired way.

2. Continue eating the daily amount of bran, even if there is increased discomfort and/or diarrhea. He said it would take from one to four weeks for the system to adjust.

3. The bran should be taken during the same four-to-six-hour period every day. For example, if a patient wanted to eat bran for breakfast, he would have to do it every day at breakfast. Or, if he preferred to divide the bran between lunch and dinner, he would have to take it every day at the same times.

4. Keep a record of daily bowel movements and any noticeable symptoms.

Bowels Respond Healthfully Within A Few Weeks. Dr. Piepmeyer reported that within a few weeks there were appreciable results. At the end of sixteen weeks, twenty-three of the thirty patients reported improvement in their symptoms. They had regular bowel movements. They had less abdominal distention and cramping. Of these twenty-three, seventeen continued using bran every day. Six use it three or four times a week. Four patients could not continue with the treatment because bran was "unpalatable." (They preferred the tortuous pains of abdominal distress, instead of a whole-grain cereal!) Only three patients out of the thirty who began this all-natural bran treatment showed no improvement. But the majority did respond to a form of relief and healing of "irritable bowel syndrome" and had few further complaints.

Natural Bran Is Recommended. Dr. Piepmeyer took time to tell his patients that there would be an "adjustment period" of from one to four weeks when taking bran. Once this hurdle was passed, hope for recovery was strong. Dr. Piepmeyer also recommended natural bran. He emphasized "the uniqueness of unprocessed bran versus other cereal products."

Dr. Piepmeyer adds that there was "a marked decrease in abdominal distention and cramps, which was associated with some decrease in anxiety."

HOW BRAN CREATES ITS NATURAL HEALING POWER

You have at times, doubtless, chewed raw wheat germ or natural bran and noted the slippery quality that develops when chewing. This is the soothing property referred to. It is unchanged by the digestive fluids and passes down the entire digestive tract unchanged. Thus it lubricates the irritated intestinal wall.

Bran is also hygroscopic in that it retains moisture in the intestinal waste. Through lubrication and moisture retention, it lessens resistance to the intestinal current.

The supply of minerals and cellulose in bran stimulates the musculo-nervous mechanism of the intestine, increasing the propulsive force back of the intestinal waste. If the bran diet is continued this lessening of resistance to the intestinal current in front and increasing the propulsive force back of the intestinal waste will help relieve almost all cases of constipation.

If you are troubled with a spastic irritation the soothing, bland, demulcent qualities of bran help to relax the spasms and permit a normal movement.

When you eat sufficient bran, you provide your bowels with the roughage that stimulates muscular activity to create regularity. Bran also offers minerals that will both stimulate and support nervous control of those muscles to keep them working efficiently for regularity.

Bran would appear to be the natural way to establish regularity and build better bowel-intestinal health.

HOW REGULARITY HOLDS THE KEY
TO BETTER HEALTH WITH BRAN

Leading nutritionist, Dr. Jean Mayer of Harvard University, in a column on bran and fiber (September 3, 1975), tells us that a low-fiber diet will produce smaller and harder wastes. Furthermore, Dr. Mayer says, "There is reason to believe that after years of hard straining and tight contractions to push chronically small, hard stools along, the intestinal muscles become overdeveloped in some spots and thin and weak in areas where the two sets come together.

"Tiny pouches, called diverticula, form in these areas. When these pouches fill with bits of feces and become infected, diverticulitis develops."

Dr. Mayer refers to studies in England demonstrating that in a high bran diet that creates sufficient roughage there is relief of the symptoms of diverticulitis in many patients. "It tends to prevent, or at least delay, its recurrence."

The British physician, Denis Burkitt, M.D., has found that a high-bran-fiber-creating diet can help protect against intestinal disorders. In commenting on this finding, Dr. Mayer says, "Dr. Burkitt and other researchers suggest that a slow-moving stool contains increased numbers of the normal intestinal bacteria that break down bile acids and thus release some cancer-producing substances.

"In a small, hard stool, these carcinogens are more concentrated, move more slowly, and have more time to work their way into the intestine. Hence, Dr. Burkitt believes that a low-fiber diet is linked to a higher incidence of intestinal cancer."

Dr. Jean Mayer feels that "adding more fiber to the typical American diet is a good thing."

Writing in the *British Medical Journal* (April 15, 1972), Dr. Burkitt says, "The dramatic rise in the incidence of diverticulosis has occurred only in economically developed countries. . . . Natives who stay on traditional eating habits (high in bran fiber) do not have the problem. . . .

The greatest contrast is to be seen between the Western world . . . and rural Africa. During 20 years of practicing surgery in Africa, Dr. Burkitt encountered not a single case of diverticulitis, nor did his surgical colleagues see the condition."

It is also acknowledged that with the problems of pollution and stress, civilized man can fall victim to digestive disorders traced to these unhealthy conditions. But there is visible evidence that bran can help in the treatment of intestinal disorders.

Dr. Burkitt says that a high-residue diet (that is, high in fiber from sources such as bran) can help correct problems of diverticular diseases.

Suggested Program. Dr. Burkitt says, "Ideally, a high-residue diet, or more correctly, an unrefined [natural] one, should include plenty of fresh fruit, vegetables and, most important of all, whole-grain bread and flours. Our ancestors, who did not get diverticulosis, ate this bread in quantity and consumed much less refined sugar."

Other good foods include whole-grain cereals to which bran can be added, vegetables such as carrots, cabbage, beets, broccoli, celery, brussels sprouts, peas, and most citrus and other fruits. It is easy to eat a variety of these tasty foods daily to provide your body with the needed roughage to maintain intestinal health.

Bran should be taken daily, since it is the food most often recommended by physicians as a chief source of fiber and roughage.

HOW BRAN HELPS CORRECT DIVERTICULOSIS

What Is It? Diverticulosis is the presence of small bulges or pockets at weak points in the large intestine. It is an ailment of the large bowel (colon) in which small pouches (diverticula) on its inner surface become packed with wastes, then irritated and inflamed, and sometimes causing abscesses.

Actually, these small pouches or diverticula, do not cause much difficulty. But when food particles become lodged in these small sacs, along with bacteria, then inflammation may result and this causes diverticulosis.

How Diverticulosis Is Caused. An explanation is made by Denis Burkitt, M.D., and Dr. Neil Painter in the *British Medical Journal* (May 22, 1971). To begin, the doctors explain that waves of muscular contraction (known as peristalsis) move waste matter through the sacs of the lower intestine. When the bowels are full of this waste matter, the muscles enveloping the intestines contract slightly to move it along.

The problem of lack of sufficient roughage or fiber, such as insufficient bran in the diet, means that the muscles are forced to contract with greater vigor to create the pressure to keep things moving. These intense contractions cause difficulty. They occur largely in the sigmoid colon (that segment of the colon that leads directly into the rectum) which is rather narrow but lined with strong muscles.

These contractions cause the build up of tremendous pressure; the bowel is often incapable of coping with such pressure. A risk here is that the bowel lining bursts through the surrounding muscles and forms a balloon or diverticulum. Over a period of time, many of these diverticula form, especially in the narrow sigmoid colon.

The basic cause of formation of diverticula is the lack of sufficient bran-created fiber, roughage, or cellulose in the diet. Doctors Burkitt and Painter have found that in people who eat a high-bran or roughage diet, the sigmoid colon muscles can contract with normal muscular force and there is little risk of bursting the bowel lining. The key to prevention of the formation of diverticulosis is to supply adequate bran to the diet so there is sufficient roughage.

THE HEALTH RISK OF THE LOW-RESIDUE DIET

A soft, low-residue or "low bulk" diet is a health risk and actually contributes to diverticulosis and other bowel-intestinal disorders.

This problem was described at length by Franz Goldstein, M.D., Chief of the Department of Gastroenterology at Lankenau Hospital of Philadelphia. In the *Journal of the American Dietetic Association* (June, 1972). Dr. Goldstein said, "Low-residue diets tend to constipate. In chronic colonic afflictions, especially in ulcerative colitis, the irritable bowel syndrome, and diverticular disease, low-residue diets, though frequently prescribed, are clearly counterproductive and are actually contraindicated in the latter two conditions.

Dr. Goldstein reported that the facts about diet and diverticulitis also related to "the extremely common functional disorder known as 'spastic colon' or the 'irritable bowel syndrome.' " This latter disorder may be a forerunner of diverticular disease. Dr. Goldstein said that "the two conditions often cannot be differentiated on clinical or radiological grounds and seem to blend into one another until the complication of diverticulitis arises."

Therefore, a low-residue diet or one that has little or no roughage can be a health risk and lead to constipation, colonic afflictions, colitis, and diverticular diseases.

Basic Corrective Remedy. To protect against "spastic colon" or diverticulitis and related disorders, a high-roughage diet forms a basic corrective remedy. Bran, lots of seeds and nuts (thoroughly chewed so they can be easily digested), raw fruits and vegetables, help provide the needed fiber to protect against these problems.

Bran Is Most Helpful. Many persons troubled with a "spastic colon" or diverticulosis, find that roughage may irritate the bowels. Improperly chewed seeds were swallowed and often lodged in the sacs of the intestine. This created discomfort. Therefore, a low-roughage diet was often followed to ease this problem. But this worsened the risk of colitis and diverticulosis, too. Recently, it was found that bran is the natural and safe way to provide roughage without the risk of irritation. *The reason is that bran, the outer coating of the wheat kernel, when thoroughly chewed or otherwise liquefied, provides the much-needed roughage with little or no irritation.*

The Healing Power of Bran. The unique and special healing power of bran is described by T. G. Parks, M.D., a surgeon, in the *Proceedings of the Royal Society of Medicine* (Vol. 66, July, 1973).

Dr. Parks told twenty patients with diverticular disease of the colon to take a small amount of bran every day. It came to about 10 grams, or about one-third of an ounce. (This is slightly more than one tablespoon.) Previously, the patients had been on a "standard low-residue diet." Dr. Parks told them to continue taking this one-third of an ounce of bran daily.

In a short time the patients had regular bowel movements. Then he increased the bran intake to 95 grams and then up to 175 grams per day (about 6 ounces).

The results were even better since the wastes consisted of over 80 per cent water. In many cases of diverticulosis, there is a noticeable lack or absence of water.

Dr. Parks reported that bran in the intestine helps absorb much needed water to create regularity. But, as Dr. Parks noted, *bran actually absorbs about eight times its own weight in water,* which he says, "results in the passage of more bulky, softer stools, particularly in patients previously troubled with constipation."

Dr. Parks suggests that daily bran intake would help create normal bowel movements to help prevent formation of high-pressure segments of the bowel from which diverticula can explode!

HOW BRAN WAS USED AS A NATURAL REMEDY FOR DIVERTICULAR DISEASE

Doctors Neil S. Painter and Anthony Z. Almeida, doctors associated with London's Manor House Hospital, and another physician, Kenneth W. Coleburne, worked as a team to treat some seventy patients who had *severe diverticular disease of the colon.*

Reporting to the *British Medical Journal* (April 15, 1972), the doctors tell of prescribing this simple program: "*The patients were told to take unprocessed, natural bran every single day. They were told to eat lots of fruits, vegetables, whole grain breads for additional sources of fiber and roughage. They were told to reduce their intake of refined sugar in any form."*

Symptoms Are Relieved. The doctors report their patients experienced relief of such symptoms as constipation, severe colic, stomach pain, tender rectum, heartburn, nausea, bloated feeling, and incomplete evacuation of the rectum. About 80 per cent who complained of previously having to strain at the stool no longer had this problem.

Regularity Established. The doctors reported that bran helped every one of the patients where regularity was established; one bowel movement at least once daily.

Bran Normalizes Intestinal System. Most interesting is that bran helped patients who had problems of diarrhea; namely, bran helped establish a normal intestinal condition to relieve and heal abnormal bowel movements. Bran, therefore, has this unique ability to correct problems of constipation as well as diarrhea.

Bran Eliminated Need for Surgery. The doctors say that many of these patients, who were an average age of sixty, had such severe pain and bowel problems that they were being considered for surgery. But the described all-natural bran diet eliminated the need for surgery.

BRAN HELPS PROTECT AGAINST VARICOSE VEINS

An ailment often related to constipation or straining is varicose veins. There appears to be a connection between intestinal disorders and varicose veins, according to C. Latto, M.D. of the Royal Berkshire Hospital of Reading, England. This condition can also be eased and even erased with a daily intake of bran.

Dr. Latto, in an article entitled, "Diverticular Disease

and Varicose Veins," in *Lancet* (May 19, 1973), says that both of these ailments are often caused by a low-fiber diet. He notes that people who eat a high-fiber diet (such as bran) rarely, if ever, have either diverticular disease or varicose veins.

The team of physicians headed by Dr. Latto treated a group of patients with varicose veins. An examination showed that 74 percent of these patients also had diverticular disease. *They explain that people who have diverticular disease are more than twice as likely to develop varicose veins as other folks.*

Dr. Latto and his colleague offer various explanations for the association of these two ailments. They say that the raised pressure created within the colon as the muscles contract with abnormal strength to expel too-small stools "is known to be transmitted down the leg veins after the valves become incompetent." A plausible explanation for this condition is that this pressure on the veins passing through the pelvis causes a back-up of blood flow. The result is often a combination of diverticulitis and varicose veins.

Fiber Could Protect Against Problem. Bran, a prime source of fiber, could offer the needed roughage to create better bowel health so that either or both of these two problems could be avoided or eased.

Natural Bran Is Best. In almost all reported cases, doctors preferred the use of unprocessed, natural bran for best results. It is free of additives or sugar, easily enjoyed, and a powerful source of the needed fiber to normalize intestinal and bowel health.

HOW BRAN MAY HELP GUARD AGAINST INTESTINAL SURGERY

The problem of diverticulitis as well as related intestinal infection is often too easily "solved" by surgery. Basically, diverticular disease may be traced to either too-powerful contractions of the bowel, or of inflammation of the sacs or pockets. (This is traced to the lodging of food waste in the sacs.) Often, the sacs may perforate; this creates a highly dangerous condition. Toxic waste matter of the bowels may seep into the bloodstreams to create a form of poisoning!

When bowel pain occurs, if there is the threat of a serious infection, doctors often recommend surgery.

But there are many doctors who prefer not to rush into colonic surgery if it can be avoided. One such doctor, Adam N. Smith, M.D., consultant surgeon at the University of Edinburgh, Scotland, told of his beliefs before the fifth biennial congress of the International Society of Colon and Rectal Surgery. As reported in *Medical World News,* (June 21, 1974), diverticular disease is rampant in those countries, or amongst those people on a low-fiber diet.

Dr. Smith says that a high-residue or high-fiber diet helps bulk up waste matter in the colon—a result of absorbing large amounts of water. When the colon contracts when there is added bulk (this is called intestinal motility) it need not do so with hard contractions. Neither must the colon force a high pressure in order to expel small hard waste matter. Instead, a high-fiber diet can actually normalize the colon and make movement a comparatively pressure-free reaction.

Dr. Smith says, "If high intraluminal pressure [inside the segments of the colon] is one of the predisposing factors in the genesis of diverticular disease, it follows that [surgical] operations for this condition may be judged effectively in terms of colonic motility."

Surgery Offers No Therapy. Dr. Smith tells of examining patients who had a colon resection (a surgical consequence wherein a portion of an incompetent tract is removed). Dr. Smith found that surgery still did not influence the pressure or vigor of the colon.

"This shows that the abnormality of the muscle in diverticular disease is generalized and is not affected by removing the sigmoid colon." (The sigmoid colon is that portion that leads directly to the rectum and the source of the most powerful contractions.)

Even after surgery was performed, there was only a temporary correction of the problem. Within a few years, diverticular disease returned.

Bran Is Used As Therapy. Dr. Smith put a group of patients on a daily dose of 20 grams of unprocessed or natural bran, together with the normal diet. (This comes to 4 tablespoons of bran a day.) After five years of observation, *Dr. Smith reported that this bran diet kept the abnormal colon pressure down—during all the years of observation.*

Dr. Smith also says that under the bran therapy, "the colonic activity fell even lower than it did with myotomy [surgery] alone. In light of our findings we advise giving patients bran after either a resection or a myotomy."

May Be Natural Cure. Doctors Painter, Almeida, and Colbourne also tell of giving seventy patients with diagnosed diverticular disease, a daily dose from one teaspoonful to 9 tablespoonsful of bran every single day. It is said that 90 percent were able to relieve or completely abolish their symptoms—which ranged from heartburn to nausea to severe colic to constipation.

But more important, the doctors say that bran may well be a natural cure. *"Twelve patients who suffered from painful diverticular disease had recurrent attacks of severe colic and might well have come to surgery . . . in four, the colic was relieved. In seven, it was abolished by the bran diet. None came to surgery despite the fact that formerly they had had attacks of severe pain. One woman of 50 had had three attacks of left renal colic . . . she was placed on the bran diet and had no further pain for two years. Occasionally, she experienced mild cramp. This disappeared when she doubled her intake of bran for a few days. Thus even severe pain which might have led to surgery will respond to a high-residue diet!"*

Effectiveness Of Bran. This fiber-creating food is NOT a laxative. Rather, it tends to *normalize* and *regulate* the actions of the bowels. It is able to help halt chronic constipation and halt chronic diarrhea. When you add bran to your diet, you help restore your bowels to their natural function.

Bran Is Not Scratchy. Dr. Painter says, "In not one of the sixty-two patients was the appetite made worse by bran. This suggests that the widely held view that so-called 'roughage' irritates the gut is not founded on fact; bran when moist becomes 'softage.'"

Bran is different from many other high-fiber foods. *Bran has the ability to absorb many times its own weight in water.* The consistency of water-swollen bran is somewhat like that of a sponge. Therefore, you should take bran with lots of liquids. This could be fruit or vegetable juice, milk, tea, soup, etc. You may also add bran to your meat loaves, casseroles, stews, but your meal should be accompanied by much fluid so the bran can become "swollen" with water and create normalization of the intestinal canal.

Begin your bran intake slowly and then gradually increase the amount so as to give your body a chance to adjust. Again, it is important to use natural and *unprocessed bran.* The doctors all used this form of bran. They do not recommend the commercial cereal-type bran, which is not only processed and saturated with chemicals and additives, but is also loaded with sugar. To rebuild natural bowel health, use natural and unprocessed bran, which is available in most health stores.

Dr. Denis Burkitt says that in his household, an 8-gram spoonful of bran is added to each person's food every day. The Burkitts also eat whole grain bread daily. This could be a good guideline for most people.

BRAN HELPS RELIEVE OTHER PROBLEMS

Doctors Neil S. Painter, Anthony Z. Almeida and Kenneth W. Coleburne reported to the *British Medical Journal* that bran helped relieve other problems such as:

• **Constipation.** Under daily bran intake, constipation could be either relieved or abolished.

• **Severe Colic.** A daily intake could both relieve and abolish this disorder.

• **Abdominal Pain.** A daily bran supplement could relieve and abolish stomach pain.

• **Tender Rectum.** Nearly all patients found that bran relieved and eventually abolished this problem.

How Much To Take? The doctors prescribed amounts ranging from one small spoonful daily to 3 tablespoons 3 times daily. The average was about 2 teaspoons of bran, 3 times a day. Each person needs to set his own rate. The doctors also note that there may be some distention felt at the very start. So it would be best to begin slowly and gradually increase amount—always with a lot of liquids.

While fiber is also available in fruits, vegetables, nuts, seeds, and other grains, bran is best because it absorbs great amounts of water and therefore produces larger and softer stools

In the words of Doctors Painter and Burkitt, "Diverticular disease is a deficiency disease, and like scurvy, it should be avoidable."

DIETARY FIBER AND DISEASE

Doctors Denis P. Burkitt, A. R. P. Walker, and Neil S. Painter, writing in the *Journal of the AMA* (Aug. 19, 1974), tell us, "Many diseases common in and characteristic of modern western civilization have been shown to be related to the amount of time necessary for the passage of intestinal content through the alimentary tract, and to the bulk and consistency of stools. These factors have in turn been shown to be greatly influenced by the fiber content of the diet and by the amount of cereal fiber [bran] in particular.

"Mechanisms are postulated whereby these changes in gastrointestinal behavior could in part explain the occurrence of such common disorders as ischemic heart disease [loss of blood supply to the heart because of blood vessel damage], appendicitis, diverticular disease, gall bladder disease, varicose veins, deep vein thrombosis, hiatus hernia, and tumors of the large bowel.

"Calorie intake, speed of passage through the intestine, levels of intracolonic pressures, number and type of fecal bacteria, as well as levels of serum cholesterol and changes in bile-salt metabolism *have all been shown to be related to the amount of dietary fiber consumed."*

The doctors say that fruits and vegetables, while most certainly important in the diet, do provide "much less effect on bowel physiology than does cereal [bran] fiber."

This means that bran is the undisputed leading food for fiber.

Unprocessed bran, say the doctors, also help speed up the transit time of a bowel movement, and this is the key to better intestinal health.

Diverticular Disease of the Colon. The doctors say, "We believe this to be a deficiency caused by lack of fiber in the diet that results from the refining of carbohydrate foods. This conclusion is consistent with the evidence that the disease is almost unknown in communities where individuals eat a high-residue diet, that a high-residue diet relieves symptoms in the majority of patients, and that the condition can be produced experimentally by feeding animals a low-residue diet."

This simple, every day food element—all-natural, drugless—is hailed by physicians throughout the world as a miracle substance that can help rebuild your bowels and intestines—and add years to your life, too!

CHAPTER 4

HOW BRAN CAN ADD YEARS
TO YOUR HEART

Latest estimates indicate that in the United States alone more than 28 million are afflicted with cardiovascular ailments that are responsible for more than one million fatalities each year. This represents more fatalities than for all other causes combined. Heart attack is the nation's number one killer. To understand how bran and fiber can add years to your heart, let us take a closer look at this health threat known as a heart attack.

Heart Attack: The Big Build-up. No heart attack is ever really "sudden." It may just seem that way to the victim and members of his family. Coronary disease has in all likelihood been building over the years, helped along by the victim who has ignored the risk factors and failed to heed the early warning signs.

Usually, when we speak of a heart attack, we mean a sudden blocking of one of the arteries that supply the heart muscle with blood.

Although the heart attack is sudden, it is the result of a slowly developing disease process (atherosclerosis) of the coronary arteries. In atherosclerosis, the passageway through the arteries becomes roughened and narrowed by fatty deposits.

When this happens, a blood clot (thrombus) may form in the narrowed artery and block the flow of blood to the part of the heart muscle supplied by the artery. The result is heart attack, which is also called coronary thrombosis, coronary occlusion, or myocardial infarction. (In myocardial infarction, that part of the heart muscle supplied by the blocked artery does not get enough oxygen and other nutrients and begins to die.)

To enable the damaged heart muscles to heal, small blood vessels open up to detour more blood through the damaged area. This is called collateral circulation. It is the heart's own life-saving method in which other blood vessels take over the functions of the blocked artery. As healing progresses, part of the injured muscle may be replaced by scar tissue.

The collateral circulatory system may also be evident long before a heart attack occurs as these detours open up to take on some of the functions of coronary blood vessels narrowed by atherosclerosis.

In other types of heart attack a wandering blood clot (embolus) may travel through the arterial channel until it reaches a narrow point where it wedges and forms a dam.

Narrow but unclogged coronary arteries may not be able to deliver the additional oxygen required in emotional excitement or severe physical exertion, and this may lead to a serious or even fatal disruption of heart rhythm.

When the heart fails to get enough blood from an inadequate circulatory system to meet its oxygen needs, a warning signal short of an actual heart attack often develops. This chest pain is called angina pectoris and is indicated by a sensation of tightening in the chest and heavy pressure or pain behind the breastbone, sometimes radiating to the shoulder, neck, arm, hand, or back.

When angina pain strikes, physical demands on the heart must be reduced. Medication such as nitroglycerin can erase the load on the heart by dilating the vessels and improving the blood flow. But in a true heart attack the pain is usually more persistent and is unrelieved by nitroglycerin or rest.

Heart Attacks Rare, Unknown Among Primitive Peoples. A group of British physicians and researchers want to know why heart trouble afflicts people in the Western world but seems to be either rare or unknown among people of the underdeveloped parts of the world such as South America, Asia, and Africa. Doctors Hugh Trowell,

Neil Painter, and Denis Burkitt, reporting to the *American Journal of Digestive Diseases* (September, 1974), say that ischemic heart disease (blood supply to the heart is blocked) and diverticular disease of the colon are alike in many respects.

The physicians say that both of these ailments afflict the same people at the same time. It is believed that the cause may be traced to a poor or imbalanced diet.

The doctors suggest that returning to a diet of whole natural unrefined grains and other fiber-rich whole foods such as bran could do much to protect and prevent heart trouble.

When the diet is high in fiber foods, consisting of bran, and tough, undigestible parts of fruits, vegetables, and grains, there is a more regular form of intestinal health. There is "regularity." This appears to guard against intestinal ailments and also appears to adjust the body mechanism so that there is a marked reduction of the risk of heart trouble.

Survey Confirms Suspicions. The team of physicians sent questionnaires to 170 hospitals in Pakistan, India, Africa. This survey confirmed their suspicions. Namely, that both diseases—heart trouble and diverticular disease—afflict the same patient at the same time. But while such ailments are especially prevalent among Westerners, they appear to be virtually absent in the more primitive portions of the world where a high-fiber intake is the general rule.

The doctors report that diverticular disease strikes about four out of every ten English people over the age of sixty. This same ailment afflicts most people who also have heart disease. The doctors tell of a survey wherein they found that in Northern Europe, the United States, and Canada, the problem of heart disease is so great (as the leading cause of death) that it "threatens to become the greatest epidemic mankind has ever faced."

Fiber Makes the Difference. The doctors note that in South Africa three out of every ten white people who eat very little fiber have diverticular disease and that their incidence of heart disease is the highest in the world.

On the other hand, among the black Africans who eat a high-fiber diet, ischemic disease is almost unknown! In African hospitals not one case of diverticular disease in natives has been seen in 120 hospitals. *The doctors queried 94 hospital doctors who said they had never seen a case of heart disease among the fiber-eating African natives.*

But the African natives who live in cities and eat the low-fiber Western diet are beginning to show more and more cases of heart attacks together with diverticular diseases!

So it is obvious that fiber does make the difference in protecting against these ailments and killers!

Low-Fiber Countries Higher in Heart Trouble. The doctors note that in those countries where there is low-fiber intake, there is a corresponding higher rate of heart trouble. In England, diverticular disease and heart trouble are twenty times more prevalent than during the preceding century. In the United States, death from heart disease leaped from 79 million people in 1930 to 2,900 per million in 1963 (and the rate is still climbing) in a "truly remarkable increase," say the doctors. It is also remarkable that both of these diseases—heart trouble with diverticular distress—appear in the same person. Even more remarkable is that these ailments are found in countries where there is a low-fiber intake.

Doctors Note These Facts. Doctors Trowell, Painter, and Burkitt tell us that a Scotsman eats about 3,450 calories a day, with only 3 grams of fiber. But a South African Bantu may not only take in more calories but also will take as much as 25 grams of fiber a day!

The Scotsman eats bleached white bread and boiled potatoes without skin, with negligible fruits and vegetables —which means very little fiber.

The Bantu may eat few fruits and vegetables, but he does have a high whole-grain cereal intake; it consists of pounded and stone-ground corn with all of its natural fiber and nutrient content.

Fiber Does Make the Difference. Reportedly, when fiber is high in the diet, there is a natural barrier against diverticular disease and there is also a natural reduction of the levels of unhealthy fatty substances in the blood. This is the natural way to help protect the heart with lower cholesterol readings.

Food fiber from bran has a biological reaction; it influences the consistency of the colon contents. Bran fiber regulates the pressure the colon must generate to propel these contents. This process appears to create better body health and resultant resistance to both diverticular disease and heart trouble.

The incidence of heart disease remarkably parallels that of diverticular disease as a life and health risk. But the doctors say that both of these diseases are rare among those people who eat a high-fiber diet. They believe that both of these degenerative diseases may be caused by a deficiency in our "internal environment." Namely, it is believed that fiber does make the difference!

The doctors say, "It is reasonable to suggest that dietary fiber, a factor that most nutritionists have ignored—may protect—at least in part—against the advent of arterial disease.

"This suggestion is supported by a large survey of Irish brothers, all of whom grew up in Ireland. Some of these brothers emigrated to the United States and ate an average of 3.6 grams of crude fiber daily. They showed nearly twice the electrocardiograph evidence of ischemic heart disease as the brothers who stayed in Ireland and ate much more animal fat but consumed an average of 6.4 grams per day of crude fiber."

Dr. Denis Burkitt, as quoted in *Prevention* (November, 1973) does say quite plainly, "I don't say that fiber deficiency is the *only* cause of coronary heart disease. But I do suggest that it may be an important factor that has been overlooked. *There is good evidence that fiber content, possibly more than any other single factor, affects cholester-*

ol levels. When dietary fiber is low, serum cholesterol levels are high. And vice versa. In non-Westernized societies where unrefined foods provide a high fiber intake, both serum cholesterol levels and the incidence of coronary heart disease are characteristically low."

Dr. Burkitt calls for a higher daily intake of bran to help protect the heart and the intestines against ill health.

How Much To Take? Dr. Burkitt suggests whole-grain breads and baked goods daily for good fiber intake. He specifically recommends 2 or 3 teaspoons of 100 percent pure bran daily as a good and all-natural fiber supplement.

It may well be the tasty, easy, and more practical way to add years to your heart.

More Benefits of Bran. Whole-grain bran is also a good source of polyunsaturates as well as vitamin E. These substances can protect the heart. Basically, the vitamin E in bran prevents the attachment of oxygen to the open bonds of the polyunsaturates. Ordinarily, polyunsaturates are oxidized by the oxygen in the body. This process forms highly toxic hydrogen peroxide as well as those heart-dangerous substances known as free radicals. (Free radicals are molecules that attack cells in the body and may cause malfunctioning of the heart.) But the vitamin E in bran helps protect against this occurrence. By adding fiber to your daily diet, you can feast your way to a longer heart life-span.

OTHER FACTORS TO IMPROVE YOUR HEART'S HEALTH

The American Heart Association points to four basic risk factors that can be changed by the person to help improve the health of the heart: These are:

1. Cigarette Smoking. Risk of heart attack and stroke increases in direct relation to the number of cigarettes smoked. A person who smokes more than one pack of cigarettes a day has nearly twice the risk of heart attack and nearly five times the risk of stroke than a nonsmoker.

2. Diet. A balanced diet low in saturated fat and cholesterol, which contains the number of calories needed to maintain optimal body weight, will help reduce the risk of heart attack and stroke and prevent overweight as well.

3. Stress. Stress is a common environmental factor that may contribute to cardiovascular disease. Only the individual himself can alter his life style and control his emotional reactions to daily events.

4. Exercise. Some studies show that people who lead sedentary lives run a higher risk of heart attack than those who get regular exercise. However, exercise programs should be undertaken only on the advice of a physician. The doctor should test the individual carefully to determine the reserve and capability of his cardiovascular system and then prescribe the appropriate kind and amount of exercise.

A TYPICAL HEART-HEALTHY, HIGH-FIBER MENU PLAN

In planning your fiber program, here is a suggested menu plan:

BREAKFAST:
Two whole oranges
Whole-grain oatmeal with bran in milk
Whole-grain toast
Poached egg
Beverage

LUNCH:
Meat or fish sandwich on whole-grain bread
Raw salad of radishes, carrots, lettuce, celery
Whole apple, pear, or seasonal fruit platter

DINNER:

Meat, poultry, or fish
Baked potatoes with skins
Tossed raw salad with many raw greens
Beverage

SNACKS:

Assorted seeds, nuts, almonds, sun-dried fruits, granola cereal with bran.

CHAPTER 5

BRAN IS A NATURAL CHOLESTEROL CONTROLLER

The cholesterol-controlling power of bran-created fiber was recognized as far back as 1954 by doctors A. R. P. Walker and U. B. Arvidsson. Writing in the *Journal of Clinical Investigation* (Vol. 33, p. 1358), the doctors point out that the high-fiber content of the essentially vegetarian diet of the South African Bantu contributed to their low cholesterol levels.

A year later doctors C. Joyner, Jr., and P. T. Kuo, writing in the *American Journal of the Medical Sciences* (Vol. 230, p. 636), explained that a diet high in fiber increases the amount of lipids or fatty substances, eliminated by the body in the wastes. Conversely, a diet low in fiber would permit retention of these fats to remain in the body and thereby raise the cholesterol levels.

Doctors Joyner and Kuo explain that fiber contains plant sterols. These are substances with a structure similar to that of cholesterol. These plant sterols in fiber appear to help regulate the level of cholesterol in the body. In particular, bran-created fiber contains both beta and gamma sitosterol, two substances that have a definite cholesterol-lowering effect in the body.

More recently, Dr. David Kritchevsky of the Wistar Institute of Philadelphia, announced that fiber works in the intestinal tract to bind bile salts that are produced from cholesterol. The bound bile salts are then excreted by the body. In a sense, it is as if the fiber "arrested" the bile salts and led them away.

Benefit of Fiber. The beneficial effect of this is that the body then makes more bile salts from stored reserves of cholesterol. The net result is a significant lowering of cholesterol in the blood. But fiber from bran, especially, is needed to create this cholesterol-controlling process.

Another benefit is described by doctors Jeremiah Stamler and Ancel Keys in *Lancet* (January, 1975) where they note that low-fiber intake could cause colonic cancer.

The doctors say that colonic cancer might be caused "in some individuals [where] the intestines were more extensively colonized with bile-degrading bacteria, perhaps as a result of a higher intake of polyunsaturated fat or a lower intake of fiber." So it would appear that cholesterol control and higher fiber intake could help create better resistance to colonic cancer. Fiber influences what happens to other elements in metabolism and may well be the most important substance available in foods.

Fiber Controls Cholesterol. Reported experiments show that the quantity of fiber in the diet can influence the amount of cholesterol in the blood. It is said that those who enjoy a high-fiber diet also have lower levels of cholesterol. Bran-created fiber appears to have a direct effect on those digestive compounds that control the levels of cholesterol. It would appear to be the long-sought-after answer for a natural way to help control cholesterol.

Dr. H. Trowell, writing in the *American Journal of Clinical Nutrition* (25; 926–32, 1972), that the case for whole grains such as bran has been strengthened with the belief that larger amounts of natural carbohydrates which are taken with their full complement of fiber (bran) is protective against excessive blood fats, such as cholesterol. Dr. Trowel explains that *bran, as a dietary fiber, decreases the reabsorption of bile salts and increases the excretion. Since bile salts constitute a pathway by which the body can rid itself of excess cholesterol, this would tend to reduce excesses of cholesterol in the blood.*

Doctor Burkitt Agrees. As quoted in *Prevention* (November, 1973), Dr. Denis Burkitt agrees. He says, "Dr. Hugh Trowell has reinterpreted certain dietary experiments designed for other purposes and has shown that, regardless of other dietary considerations, *cholesterol level falls when more fiber is consumed and rises when fiber consumption is reduced."*

Just exactly how dietary fiber creates this magical influence on regulation of serum cholesterol is still under study, but a clue could be in its effect on bile acids. Dr. Burkitt says, "There is evidence that more bile acids are excreted in large stools characteristic of a high-fiber, high-residue diet."

Bran: Key to Cholesterol Regulation. How is it believed to work? Basically, let us understand that cholesterol, either made in the body or from foods, creates bile acids. Specifically, liver cholesterol will make bile acids which are sent through the bile duct into the top portion of the small intestine, or duodenum. Here, these bile acids work to break down dietary fats. When this is done, some bile acids travel down the intestinal tract and are given off in wastes. But much of the bile acids are reabsorbed into the body, transported back to the liver via the bloodstream!

Therefore, you can see that a substance that increases excretion of bile acids might also lower serum cholesterol levels. The clue here is that as long as a sufficient amount of reabsorbed bile acids are returned to the liver, the body lowers its need to create more cholesterol. Therefore, cholesterol that would ordinarily have been used for bile acid synthesis is not metabolized in this fashion but remains in the system.

But if there is a deficiency of fiber which influences the levels of bile acid, then there is a reduction in the efficiency of the process by which cholesterol leaves the body (through catabolic metabolism into bile acids) and blood fats may increase in the body.

Also, according to Dr. Burkitt, *a high-fiber content in the intestines helps control the amount and absorption of cholesterol taken in foods.*

Therefore, as described earlier, primitive peoples who have a high-residue or high-fiber diet are benefited by the excretion of both the catabolized cholesterol (present as bile acids) and ingested cholesterol.

THE FIBER-CHOLESTEROL RELATIONSHIP

Dr. Hugh Trowell also tells of experiments that determine the fiber-cholesterol relationship. He states that when test animals were fed ground whole cereals rich in bran, their cholesterol levels fell. But when the animals were given chemical cellulose instead of natural fiber, their cholesterol level rose!

This suggests that natural bran, natural fiber, natural cellulose can control cholesterol, rather than chemical substances!

Dr. Trowell also tells of experiments in which animals were fed a hypercholesteremic diet (high fat) of whole eggs, among other foods, but were also given ground corn, barley, wheat, oats—the doctor noted that their cholesterol was reduced! Therefore, these fiber-creating grains have this unique power.

Dr. Trowell tells of humans who are able to reduce their serum cholesterol levels from 258 milligrams to 226 milligrams when put on a food program of high-fiber whole grains daily.

No doubt there are many multiple and interrelated causes of cholesterol increase. A good dietary program, together with high bran intake, would be at the forefront of a cholesterol-controlling goal.

Here is such a program as recommended by the Nutrition Clinic of the American Health Foundation.

FAT-CONTROLLED, LOW-CHOLESTEROL EATING PLAN

I. RESTRICT THESE FOODS. They contain large amounts of saturated fat and/or cholesterol and tend to raise the blood cholesterol level.

1. Fatty cuts of beef, lamb, pork and ham, hamburger, prime ribs, luncheon meats, cold cuts, frankfurters, bacon, sausage, and spare ribs.

2. Fat-rich dairy products such as cheese, whole milk, ice-cream, butter, cream, and whipped toppings.

3. Most commercially prepared cakes, pies, danish pastry, donuts, corn muffins, cookies, potato chips, and snack crackers.

4. Egg yolks, organ meats, and coconut.

5. Fried foods cooked in lard or vegetable shortening.

II. FOLLOW THESE BASIC GUIDELINES FOR DAILY EATING.

1. Use more fish, poultry, and lean meat. Limit the total amount daily to 6 to 8 ounces, cooked weight.

2. Use low-fat cheeses, skim milk, and margarine made from a polyunsaturated vegetable oil.

3. Try fresh fruit instead of fat-rich desserts.

4. Limit egg yolks to 2 per week. (Egg whites need not be limited.)

5. Use organ meats once or twice a month, as a substitute for meats.

6. Reduce the total amount of fat eaten.

7. Substitute some polyunsaturated oil, mayonnaise, or margarine listing liquid corn, safflower, or soybean oil as the first ingredient, for some of the saturated (animal) fat. Depending on how many calories you can afford, use 1 to 4 tablespoons daily.

8. Choose a balanced diet that includes such low-fat foods as leafy, green, and yellow vegetables, citrus fruits, whole-grain breads and cereals.

9. Maintain your ideal weight by controlling total calories. Overweight results from eating too much food and usually too much fat.

FOODS TO USE IN THE FAT-CONTROLLED, LOW-CHOLESTEROL EATING PLAN.

These foods are LOW in saturated fat and cholesterol:

POULTRY AND FISH

- Choose chicken, turkey and Rock Cornish hens.
- Reduce the fat in poultry by removing the skin before cooking.
- Eat fresh and salt water fish often.

LEAN CUTS OF BEEF, VEAL, LAMB

- Buy meat with very little marbling.
- Trim off fat before cooking.
- These are lean cuts of beef: sirloin steak, round steak, flank steak, beef fillet, top round, sirloin tip, rump roast.
- Buy only extra lean ground beef for hamburger.
- Lean cuts of lamb—leg chops or loin chops.
- Most veal is a good choice since it is young beef and there is usually little marbling fat.

DAIRY PRODUCTS

- Low-fat cheeses—farmer, pot, cottage, skim milk ricotta, skim milk.
- Skim milk yoghurt.
- Skim milk, buttermilk, 99 per cent fat-free milk.
- Do NOT use most nondairy milk and cream substitutes, as they contain coconut oil (high in saturated fat). Check labels carefully and choose those made from a polyunsaturated oil such as soybean oil.

FRUITS

Each day include one serving of fruit high in vitamin C, such as an orange, ½ grapefruit, lemon, lime, tangerine, cantaloupe, strawberries.

These foods contain almost *no* saturated fat and *no* cholesterol.

LEGUMES

Legumes are dried peas, beans, and nuts.

Use as meat substitutes or meat extenders in soups, baked dishes and salad.

Legumes are high in protein, high in fiber, low in fat, and contain no cholesterol.

GRAINS

Include whole-grain or enriched breads, cereals, pastas, and rice. These are good sources of fiber, along with B-complex vitamins, iron, and protein.

Feature bran daily.

Also include bagels, English Muffins, bialys.

VEGETABLES

Vegetables contain no fat, no cholesterol, and are low in calories. They are a good source of fiber, vitamin A, vitamin C, and minerals. Include two or more servings of green or deep yellow vegetables in your diet every day.

Use them raw, steamed, or baked.

FATS

- Use polyunsaturated vegetable oils: safflower, corn, sesame, cottonseed, and soybean oils.
- Use margarines listing *liquid* vegetable oil as the first ingredient.
- Use margarine or liquid vegetable oil in place of shortening in recipes.
  Vegetable shortenings are partially hydrogenated and contain less polyunsaturated oil.

Desserts
- Fresh fruits or fruit canned without sugar (helps keep calories down.)

- Cakes, pies, cookies made with polyunsaturated fat in place of solid shortening.
- Cakes made from egg whites, such as angel food cake.
- Puddings made with skim milk.
- Sherbet.

NOTE: Such a program not only helps control your intake of fat and cholesterol, it controls calories and builds general health, too.

Denis Burkitt, M.D., also agrees, as he states in the *Journal of the AMA* (Aug. 19, 1974), "Evidence is accumulating that shows that the removal of fiber from the diet raises serum cholesterol levels, a process that predisposes to coronary heart disease. *Intake of food rich in fiber and the addition of cellulose to the diet have been shown to protect against hypercholesterolemia.*

"There is some evidence that a high-residue diet increases fecal excretion of bile acids. This may account for the close association between coronary disease and diverticular disease, both being related to the consumption of refined carbohydrate foods."

Summing it up, Dr. Burkitt offers these conclusions about the importance of bran-created fiber in the diet: "Many of the diseases of Western civilization have appeared only in the last century. We believe that they owe their origin, at least in part, to the removal of indigestible fiber from the carbohydrate foods that constitute the major part of our diet.

"In the past, the physiological function of this fiber has been almost completely ignored, probably because it contributes no calories and has scarcely any nutritional value. This should be questioned, as cereal fiber is necessary not only for the 'bulk' it provides in the intestine but also for its effect on the chemical and bacteriological processes that take place in the intestine.

"Evidence has been presented to show that its removal from the diet may, directly or indirectly, cause certain diseases that are becoming an increasing problem in Western countries."

Cholesterol and Coronary Connection. In *Lancet* (December 30, 1972), Denis Burkitt, M.D., offers the connection between these problems, as prompted by a low-fiber intake.

Dr. Burkitt says, "The serum-cholesterol rises when fiber is removed from the diet. Eating a fiber-rich diet or adding cellulose to the diet lowers the serum-cholesterol.

"Diverticular disease and coronary disease are closely associated in patients, and a high-fiber diet increases the excretion of bile acids in the feces. Hence, it is possible that the removal of fiber from foodstuffs not only causes diverticulitis . . . but may also be partly responsible for the appearance of coronary-artery thrombosis.

"Some of the diseases that have become a common problem in Western countries in this century may be caused, at least in part, by the removal of dietary fiber from carbohydrate foods.

"The role of cereal fiber (such as bran) in the diet has attracted little attention, presumably because it has little energy value.

"Sufficient evidence is already available to show that fiber does not only provide 'bulk' but also in some way affects the physiological processes which occur in the gut and the bacterial flora which inhabit it.

"Fiber deficiency has been shown to be an apparent cause of diverticulosis and so may be of great importance in the causation of other diseases associated with diverticular disease. Therefore, its role in human physiology deserves more attention."

CHAPTER 6

THE TASTY WAY TO PLAN YOUR HIGH-FIBER PROGRAM

You can enjoy gourmet taste on a high-fiber program with a variety of different foods eaten with your daily meals. To begin with, the term "dietary fiber" identifies all plant material resistant to digestion by digestive juices. Plant materials include seeds, nuts, beans, fruits, and vegetables, as well as the now-familiar grains. For good health, you should have a *balance* and *variety* of these plant foods.

According to Benjamin H. Ershoff, Ph.D., of the Loma Linda University School of Medicine, "If giving people a few tablespoons of bran each day answered all the questions about fiber and cured all the diseases, we'd have no reason to continue research." Dr. Ershoff says that different types of dietary fibers have different reactions upon the system. So a *balance* will help promote good health. "Dietary fiber is not an inert substance which passes unchanged through the gastrointestinal tract," says Dr. Ershoff, "but a group of compounds that play an important role in the maintenance of health. *Different fibers have different activities and different effects.*"

Three Basic Benefits of Balanced High-Fiber Foods. Dr. Ershoff lists three basic benefits of a variety of balanced high-fiber foods:

1. A balance is necessary for normal bowel function, promoting regularity, soft stools, and a rapid transit time.

2. A balance is necessary to create hypercholesterolemic and anti-atherosclerotic properties, reducing the levels of cholesterol in the bloodstream.

3. A balance is necessary to create an antitoxic reaction within the system to protect against bacterial action and irritation in the digestive-eliminative tracts.

Dr. Ershoff, along with many other researchers in the field of fiber and health, suggest a variety of different foods for optimum health. Here are some such tasty foods that you can enjoy in your daily eating program for good health and high fiber:

NUTS

A nut is defined as a dry fruit or seed with a hard, separable shell and an edible interior kernel. Included in this definition are the commonly known nuts, as well as chestnuts and coconuts and the edible seeds such as sesame, sunflower, pumpkin.

(Peanuts are treated like nuts, but botanically speaking, they belong to the same family as lentils, split peas, beans.)

Available Everywhere. A variety of nuts can be found in almost any supermarket or health store. Domestic nuts which are tasty and very high in dietary fiber include almonds, pecans, walnuts, filberts, macadamia nuts, and pine nuts (called pignolias, if imported). Imported nuts which are delicious as well as high in fiber include Brazil nuts, pistachios, chestnuts, and cashews.

How To Buy. Nuts sold in the shell should be your preference. Cashews are almost never in a shell, when sold.) A shell offers a natural protection against chemical invasion. Nuts in a shell are *not* roasted, offer a better taste and have a high source of fiber, among other nutrients. (Peanuts are usually roasted and a label will tell you this.) Wherever possible, select shelled and unroasted nuts. Otherwise, settle for shelled and/or roasted nuts. NOTE: Nearly all shelled nuts are softened and loosened with a bleach treatment. This does not penetrate the edible portions. Discard the shell and eat the nut with good health and high fiber. Pistachio nuts are naturally cream-colored. The red color is a dye. Try to avoid these types of nuts.

About Shelled Nuts. These are usually available raw, either whole or in slivers or pieces. Almonds are usually blanched. (The edible outer skin has been removed in a hot-water bath.) Raw cashews are delicious and high in fiber. Select these instead of the greasy, salted "cocktail" cashews.

Shelled nuts are available in *plastic bags* which are subject to light degradation but enable you to verify quality. They are also available in *glass jars* so that you can see if they are plump, uniform in size and color. Preferable are shelled nuts in *vacuum-packed cans* which are guarded against light and air. Of course, with a can, you cannot judge the quality of the nuts so you must experiment until you find a store and brand that is suitable.

Preservatives Not Needed. Some manufacturers will use preservatives and/or antioxidants for nuts, which are really not needed. But if they do use such preservatives, the label should state this. You would do well to select chemical-free packaged nuts.

French-Fried Nuts. This process calls for frying nuts in a bath of heavy grease or oil that is regularly being heated, then reheated, and, of course, heavily salted. So-called "cocktail nuts" fall into this group. They are difficult to digest, and may cause a rise in cholesterol and blood pressure because of the added fat and salt. These should be avoided.

How To Roast Your Own Nuts at Home. Spread a variety of different nuts on a baking sheet or shallow pan. Bake at 350°F. for 5 to 10 minutes or until lightly browned. TIP: To create a unique flavor, with more browning, add 1 teaspoon of polyunsaturated vegetable oil per cut of shelled nuts.

Roasting Nuts in the Shell. Spread a variety of nuts in their shells on a baking sheet or shallow pan. Bake at 350°F. for 20 to 25 minutes. When adequately roasted, you'll be able to remove the shell very easily. The nutmeat will be deliciously browned.

About Jars of Dry-Roasted Nuts. These are aimed at dieters and people concerned about fat intake. While they may contain "no oils" as labeled, they do have sugar, salt, starch MSG, vegetable gums, and preservatives. If you are cautious about chemical intake, pass these up. In a few minutes you can roast your own and enjoy a delicious taste with a high-fiber content.

HOW TO ENJOY TASTY HIGH-FIBER NUTS IN DAILY EATING

In planning your high-fiber program, feature nuts as often as possible in a variety of tasty ways. For example:

• Use chopped nuts in most baked products, such as breads, rolls, cookies, cakes, even as frostings and fillings.

• Use slivered almonds, pumpkin seeds, or chopped walnuts in any cooked cereal, steamed grains, and as a topping for a pudding.

• Make a hearty vegetable soup. Thicken it with a blend of 1 tablespoon of any nut butter (as a flour substitute) per quart of soup. You'll have a wholesome taste, a creamy broth, and a high-fiber soup!

• To any salad, add 1 tablespoon of chopped nuts.

• To a meal of brown rice and vegetables, add a handful of pine nuts or any other desired nuts.

• Sauté slivered almonds and sunflower seeds in oil and then add chopped vegetables for pan-frying. Makes a high-fiber meal that is deliciously good.

• Add chopped nuts to bean dishes. Or, add ground nuts to bean purées for a dip or patty or filling.

• Combine chopped nuts with fresh or sun-dried fruit slices for a tasty snack or dessert. Add chopped nuts to cottage cheese to eat out of the cup or as a sandwich filling.

Use chopped nuts for seafood as well as most any chopped sandwich fillings.

• Add chopped pecans and/or walnuts to maple syrup or honey and use as a syrup over waffles or pancakes or as a dessert topping.

• Add ground or finely chopped nuts to flour for use in almost any baked product.

• And, of course, nuts right from the shell or package are great for taste and high-fiber intake. Nuts may be high in calories but they offer you "satiety power," which means that the natural oils soothe your appetite and help control the urge to overeat. A handful of nuts before a meal may help you control your runaway appetite—and help you control your weight, too.

In a Nutshell: Plan to eat nuts raw. Chew them very thoroughly for better digestion and fiber reaction. Use nuts for delicious soups, in the form of a butter (peanut and cashew are popular), ground up fine to enjoy over cereals and salads, as well as in many fruit and vegetable dishes. Nuts are good for you!

SEEDS

A seed is the grain or ripened ovule of a plant, containing an embryo, and capable of germination. It is a prime source of many nutrients and also a major source of fiber to create necessary bulk and roughage. A seed comes from the dried fruit or seed of a plant, and has, within its nucleus, the ability to perpetuate life. It is often considered the very source of life and health.

Variety of Seeds Available. In planning your high-fiber program, use seeds daily. They are available in a wide variety of tastes. You may use aniseeds, barley, buckwheat, or cantaloup seeds, caraway seeds, coriander, cucumber seeds, fig seeds, lentils, okra, rye, sesame, squash, and sunflower, to name just a few. Buy them in plastic bags or vacuum-packed cans. Select those that are *not* salted or roasted in hydrogenated fats. Use them for good eating right out of your hand or just as you would use nuts.

Watermelon Seed Tea. Boil 3 tablespoons of freshly washed watermelon seeds in a quart of water and use as a tea, sweetened with honey, flavored with a squeeze of lemon juice. You'll be able to "drink" your fiber this way.

Okra Seeds. From fresh okra, clean the seeds. You may home-roast them for eating. Or grind them to be used as a coffee substitute. Again, this is the delicious way to "drink" your fiber. The substances in the high-fiber okra plant will steep into the tea and help give you needed intestinal lubrication for "self-scrubbing."

HOW TO ENJOY HIGH-FIBER SEEDS IN DAILY EATING

Treat yourself to good taste along with high-fiber by using seeds in these gourmet ways:

• Serve assorted seeds in a cup of yoghurt.

• Sprinkle assorted seeds on a freshly baked potato.

• For waffles, biscuits, or muffins, stir seeds into blended dry ingredients before adding liquid.

• Mix honey with some seeds and nut butter for a delicious sandwich filling; or use seeds mixed into peanut butter with cheese slices for a grilled sandwich filling.

• Add seeds to meat, poultry, or seafood salads.

• Try chopped or slivered nuts in tossed vegetable salads.

• Use toasted seeds as a quick topping for any type of pie, cake, or dessert.

• Sprinkle cupcakes with seeds before baking and skip the sugary frosting.

• For a spread on crackers or celery, add finely chopped roasted seeds to cream cheese that has been blended with a little skim milk.

• Perk up your next vegetable soufflé. Add seeds along with the vegetable.

Good for Snacks. A handful of seeds can give you good taste and much fiber when you get into the healthful habit of using them for snacks. While reading, while watching TV or any idle activity, munch on seeds. They'll give you something chewy good as well as a good supply of daily fiber.

BEANS

Beans, peas, and lentils are great fiber sources. They are also valuable for providing you with vitamins and minerals as well as meatless protein.

Solid Package of Nutrition. According to the U.S. Department of Agriculture, beans are super rich in calcium, iron, phosphorus, and the B-calcium vitamins. They're also a valuable protein (22 to 24.5 per cent) and low in fat content (1 to 1.5 per cent). Per size of serving, they match meat, poultry, and fish in protein, plus containing the B vitamins, thiamine, and niacine. Beans edge out most other foods in the amount of iron per serving. Few other foods can provide such a wealth of energy and nutrition for such a small price per pound!

Fiber + Protein = Good Health. The combination of high fiber and high protein means that the cellulose is prepared by the amino acids for good bulk use in the intestinal tract. This is important since it is protein that helps metabolize the fiber into the bulk form that helps cleanse the intestinal-eliminative tracts. It is healthy to include beans in your high-fiber program.

Basic Cooking Tips. To begin, split peas and lentils may be boiled or pressure cooked without soaking. Otherwise, almost all other beans and whole peas should be soaked before cooking to take up part of the water lost in drying. This expands the cellulose of the beans and makes it ready for easier absorption into the body.

How To Clean Beans and Peas. Rinse dry beans or peas under cold running water. Discard any small stones, discolored or shriveled beans.

How To Soak: Soak dry beans and whole peas (not split peas) overnight. Cover each one cup of beans with 3 cups of water for this overnight soaking. Next day, proceed with recipe or cook in the same water until tender. TIP FOR QUICKER SOAKING: Add dry beans or whole peas to boiling water, following same proportions as above, and over high heat, bring to a boil. Let boil 2 minutes. Remove from heat. Cover pan. Let soak 1 hour. Then proceed with recipe.

Easy Way to Cook. Season with salt substitute, onion, garlic or bay leaf, if desired. Over high heat, bring to a boil. Reduce heat to medium-low. Cover and let simmer until tender, following this timetable:

TIMETABLE FOR BEAN COOKERY

Beans Or Peas, Soaked	Approximate Cooking Time
Black beans	2 hours
Black-eyed beans, peas, or cowpeas	30 minutes
Cranberry beans	2 hours
Great Northern beans	1 to 1½ hours
Kidney beans	1½ hours
Lentils (no soaking required)	25 to 30 minutes
Lima beans, large	1 hour
Lima beans, small	45 minutes
Pea beans (navy beans)	1½ hours
Peas, split (no soaking required)	45 minutes
Peas, whole	1 hour
Pinto beans	2 hours
Soybeans	1½ hours

SUGGESTION: To prevent split skins, stir beans only occasionally. To prevent foaming, add 2 tablespoons of oil to each pound of beans or peas before cooking.

Also, one cup of dry beans or peas yields 2 to 2½ cups cooked. When buying, figure that one pound of beans or peas will provide 7 to 9 one-cup servings.

Simple trimmings for serving. You don't have to dress up plain cooked beans to enjoy them. But when you want an easy change from the usual, try these ideas at serving time:

• To drained beans, add finely sliced celery or chopped green pepper or pimiento for top-notch fiber boosting. Season further with butter, margarine, or vegetable oil.

• Make a quick and tangy sauce by thinning tomato juice with an equal amount of water or the bean liquid. Add finely chopped onion. Pour the drained beans into the sauce, heat until the sauce bubbles and you have high-fiber beans, Rancho deluxe style.

• Thin a little gravy and add a pinch of a favorite seasoning such as thyme, poppy seeds, or ground cloves. Pour in the drained cooked beans and eat. Terrific taste. High-fiber source, too.

GETTING THE MOST FOR YOUR BEAN-FIBER SHOPPING DOLLAR

To find good quality beans that are high in fiber when you shop, keep these points in mind and view:

• Dried beans should have a bright, uniform color. If you see faded beans, pass them up. They have been stored too long and if used, require very long cooking processes that deplete vitamin and fiber power. Taste is poor, too.

• A package of beans should offer them in uniform size. Small beans cook faster than large ones. If you have a mixture, then the end result will be cooked small beans and partially uncooked large ones. If you cook until the large ones are done, the smaller ones will become mushy.

• Beans should be free of visible defects. If they are cracked, broken, perforated, or discolored they will not give you top fiber or nutrient content. Taste will be poor, too.

Enjoy this tasty high-fiber food as often as possible. Use beans as a meal. Or use as an accompaniment to the main course. Season with tomatoes, molasses. Try sautéed onion and garlic with beans. All cooked beans can be marinated in a simple oil and vinegar dressing, then served as a delicious high-fiber salad. Add chopped scallions and parsley for additional taste. And, of course, bean soup is a staple in the high-fiber program.

FRUITS AND VEGETABLES

Tree-ripened fruits and vine-ripened vegetables offer you a rich bounty of nutrition as well as fiber. It has long been known that fruit fibers are cleansing, while vegetable fibers are building blocks. A combination will offer you good nutrition, good taste and high fiber.

Basic Buying Tips: Plant foods should be rich in color, free of defects, as fresh as possible, as seasonal as possible. Try to get poison-free fruits that have been organically grown and free of pesticides. Otherwise, wash fruits under cold running water before using. The same applies to vegetables. Follow these basic rules:

• Buy plant foods in season when prices are low and quality is high.

• Buy only as many plant foods as you need since they perish quickly with much nutrient loss and fiber weakening.

• Pass up any damaged plant foods. Handle displayed plant foods carefully to protect against ruining them for yourself or others.

• Plant foods selected should be mature, rich in color, free of blemishes with smooth skin, and with *no* punctures or decay.

Storage Tips: Plant foods should be stored in your refrigerator (for a maximum of 3 to 5 days) until used up. If a plant food has a strong odor, cover it with a plastic bag so this odor will not penetrate other foods. Wash plant foods just before serving.

HOW TO ENJOY HIGH-FIBER PLANT FOODS IN DAILY EATING

Eat plant foods daily. Select a wide variety to keep your taste buds satisfied. To enjoy plant foods, other than eating them fresh and raw, try salads. Some suggestions are:

• Arrange on a plate a lettuce leaf, lettuce wedge, tomato wedge, cauliflowerettes.

• Toss together 1 head romaine lettuce, shredded; 1 bunch spinach, shredded; 1 bunch radishes, slices; tomato French dressing.

• Arrange on bed of lettuce one large or three small green pepper rings; fill rings with cottage cheese; surround cottage cheese with sliced radishes.

• In lettuce cup, arrange cucumber slices, thin slices of onion rings, and watercress sprigs; use yoghurt dressing.

• Tomato Fan Tans: Chill peeled tomatoes; set on stem end, slice in fourths nearly to bottom; stuff between slices with mixture of cheese, finely chopped celery, radishes, and onion juice. Serve in lettuce cup; douse with French dressing.

• Pile lightly in a lettuce cup a mixture of 3 or 4 parts finely shredded carrots, 1 part coconut flakes or shreds, whiff of grated orange rind and orange juice to moisten. Top with pinch of coconut.

• Fill a large cup with ¼-inch banana slices, dates cut in lengthwise strips, grapes. Top with a little yoghurt, garnish with walnut halves.

• Place halves of seeded honeydew melon on a plate. Fill with avocado balls and pineapple cubes. Garnish with watercress.

FOURTEEN SIMPLE SALAD DRESSINGS

1. Apply just a sprinkle of salt substitute.

2. Sprinkle lemon juice lightly.

3. Sprinkle on lemon juice and same amount of oil and salt substitute.

4. Lemon juice, a little water, honey. Shake together in a bottle.

5. A few grains of salt substitute, a bit of honey, a squeeze or two of lemon.

6. Yoghurt and lemon juice.

7. Cream cheese softened with a little lemon juice. Or use other fruit juices.

8. Yoghurt and lemon juice, even buttermilk and lemon juice.

9. Fruit juice, lemon juice, honey.

10. Cottage cheese, mashed avocado, lemon juice, salt substitute.

11. Add finely chopped vegetables that have a definite flavor or vegetable salt or powder to oil dressing or mayonnaise. Also herbs. Try dill in an oil dressing.

12. Add chopped hard-cooked egg, olives, and pimiento to mayonnaise.

13. Add rolled nut meats or nut butter to mayonnaise or cooked salad dressing.

14. Grated orange rind, lemon rind, and coconut may be added.

SERVING HIGH-FIBER RAW FRUITS

• **Fruit Appetizers.** Combine several fresh fruits in a fruit cup. Or use a combination of fresh, frozen, or canned fruits.

• **Fruit Salads.** Arrange fresh fruits or a mixture of fresh, canned, or frozen fruits on crisp greens. Serve with a tangy fruit salad dressing, mayonnaise, or a mild French dressing. Try combining fruits with other foods—crisp raw vegetables, cooked meats and poultry, cheese, nuts and cooked seafood.

• **Fruit Plates.** Arrange several fruits on a bed of crisp greens. Add cheese or sherbet. Serve with small sandwiches or whole-grain bread.

• **Fruit Snacks.** Choose fresh fruits to eat alone or with oatmeal cookies, skim milk, or cheese. Calorie watchers find that a serving of fresh fruit—an apple or an orange— often satisfies hunger without adding too many calories.

• **Fruit Garnishes.** Meat and poultry garnishes include whole cranberry sauce in orange cups; broiled peach halves; pan-broiled apple rings; pineapple spears; orange slices. For appetizers, try thin slices of lemon and lime, melon balls, large whole strawberries, grapes.

• **Fruit Desserts.** Serve fresh raw fruit singly or in combination—sweetened or unsweetened—plain or topped with skim milk, sweet cream, sour cream, whipped cream, or yoghurt, depending upon individual taste and waistlines!

HIGH-FIBER FRUIT APPETIZERS—IN MINUTES

• Dip banana chunks in lemon juice and roll in finely chopped nuts. Spear on toothpicks.
• Dip unpared apple rings and pear wedges in lemon juice and spread with a mixture of Roquefort or blue cheese and softened cream cheese.
• String on toothpicks two or more of the following: Fresh pineapple cubes, seedless grapes, whole fresh berries, pear and apple chunks (dipped in lemon juice), cantaloupe cubes, orange sections. Serve with a skim milk yoghurt dip or bleu cheese dip.
Balance your intake of fiber with a delicious variety of foods from the nut, seed, bean, and plant kingdoms. You can feast your way to good health with these all-natural, succulent, high-fiber foods.

CHAPTER 7

A LISTING OF NATURAL SOURCES OF BRAN AND FIBER

A high-bran and high-fiber food program is an exciting adventure in good taste from good foods. While there are many ways to increase daily dietary fiber, the easy way is, of course, to have a whole-bran cereal with milk and fruit slices in the morning. This is just one source of bran and fiber. Where else can you obtain fiber?

Sources Of Fiber. The most concentrated source is bran. Basically, food fiber comes from plant foods—grains, fruits, vegetables, nuts, and seeds. Also good are the granola-type cereals, wheat and oat cereals, either cooked or ready-to-eat. It is important to select all-natural cereals since doctors report that *unprocessed* bran is the most satisfactory. You may enjoy miller's bran and packaged all-natural cereals for your fiber intake. Vegetables also offer a good source of fiber. Fruit is another excellent source. It is best to eat these foods unpeeled and raw; if you must cook, do so slightly. Sun-dried fruits and nuts are good sources of high fiber, but they are higher in calories, so eat them in moderation if you are calorie counting. Also—*drink water with fiber foods. Fiber will absorb liquid and swell up, adding more needed bulk or roughage to your diet.*

Animal Foods Have No Fiber. Meat, fish, poultry, and dairy products (all are animal-source foods) have no fiber at all. They are important in your daily diet, but you should also include bran and other plant foods for your fiber and roughage.

How Much Fiber Do You Need? It is estimated that the

average person consumes about 2 or 3 grams of crude fiber each day. New medical studies suggest that you should be getting closer to 6 or 7 grams per day. While no recommended daily allowance for fiber has yet been established, it is said that the need for fiber varies with the individual. Your best guide is the effect on you of added fiber. If the amount of roughage you eat is not producing regular movements then add more fiber to your diet. If the reverse is true, reduce fiber intake. And before you make any drastic diet changes, be sure to check with your family physician.

FOURTEEN WAYS TO INCREASE BRAN-FIBER INTAKE

You can feast your way to a high bran-fiber intake with these fourteen basic suggestions. Diversify and make your own high-fiber eating programs:

1. As often as is palatable, enjoy miller's bran and packaged unprocessed bran cereal with milk or fruit juice. Also vary with the granola-type cereals, wheat and oat cereals, dry or hot. Choose the *slow-cooking* cereals for higher bran content, instead of the "instant" kind.

2. Raw vegetables, or those steamed slightly, offer you good supplies of fiber and roughage. A raw vegetable salad topped with yoghurt and sprinkled with bran flakes makes a good high-fiber meal-in-a-dish.

3. Use bran for more than a breakfast food. It can be a good dessert. TIP: Combine a portion of unprocessed bran with granola, add fresh fruit slices, a scoop of cottage cheese and/or yoghurt, a drizzle of honey and you have a high-fiber all-natural delicious dessert.

4. Transform soup into a high-fiber food by adding lots of fresh chopped or sliced raw vegetables. Also, a scoop of cottage cheese in this type of soup makes a meal-in-itself.

5. Green pea soup with bran flakes for filler, makes a high-fiber food with gourmet taste.

6. Raw fruits should be your dessert almost daily. Wash seasoned fresh fruits, slice or chop or make into an attractive platter with crackers for good fiber intake. Add chopped fruits to most salads, desserts, even to meat dishes.

7. Citrus fruits are good sources of fiber. Peel oranges, grapefruits, tangerines *but keep the fibrous membranes* to give you top-notch fiber. Use for dessert.

8. A platter of assorted seeds, nuts, and sun-dried fruits makes an excellent and tasty, crunchy-good high-fiber snack. But these foods are also calorie-high, so use in moderation.

9. Raw fresh salads are a "must" in the high-fiber program. Use all-natural salad dressings such as a mixture of apple cider, vinegar, oil, and honey. Or try a blending of cottage cheese and lemon juice, flavored with onion or garlic powder and herbs. A good and easy dressing is simple tomato juice spiked with lemon, garlic, and herbs.

10. Try a baked or steamed potato. But leave the skin on. (Wash and/or scrub it before cooking, though.) The fiber and most of the nutrients are highly concentrated in the potato's skin. Keep it low-calorie by moistening with some hot nonfat milk and chives.

11. Bolster the effectiveness of roughage by using yoghurt made from skim milk. It contains beneficial bacteria that alert roughage in the intestines to perform more efficiently. You may add fresh fruit slices to yoghurt. Also add wheat germ or a spoon of bran flakes. Stir thoroughly and then enjoy.

12. With your fiber meals, drink beverages such as fruit and vegetable juices or even water. Fiber will absorb

the liquid and swell up; this adds even more needed roughage or bulk to your diet.

13. Wherever possible, eat whole-grain foods. All breads, all grains, should be whole grain. A variety is available in most health stores as well as supermarkets.

14. New on the scene (although known to select groups of people in the world) are kasha (buckwheat groats) and bulgur wheat, or couscous. These are delicious whole-grain foods that are prime sources of bran-creating fiber. Use them as you would brown rice. You may also use brown rice as a good source of fiber.

HOW TO USE WHOLE GRAINS FOR YOUR FIBER

Doctors report that the best grains are unprocessed and as natural as possible. The less that is done to a grain the greater the retention of bran as well as vitamins, minerals, and other nutrients. When buying grains, select those that are whole; preferably, those that have not yet been cracked or ground. You may do this in these easy ways:

1. You can sprout whole grains at home, making them ready for delicious eating.

2. You may soak whole grains to make them more palatable and easier to eat. Good taste, too.

3. Cook whole grains until tender. You may then use the grains for making bread, cereals, soups, salads, casseroles, patties, cookies, and so forth.

Grains will add much taste, texture, and valuable nutrition to just about any recipe. Unprocessed bran may be enjoyed raw in almost all recipes. Good for eating with fruit slices or in yoghurt.

Whole Grain Flakes. Health stores have whole-grain flakes available. How are they made? Basically, the whole grains are quickly cooked (about 15 to 20 seconds) under dry radiant heat. Each grain acts as its own small pressure cooker. Then the grains drop into rollers and are flattened into complete whole-grain flakes. This process eliminates all refining or possible leaching of nutrients through wet methods. Health stores have whole-grain flakes, prepared as described above, available for your use.

Whole-grain flakes may be used to add taste, texture, and nutrition to breads, cakes, cereals, casseroles, soups, sauces, dips, stews. (Flakes are lightweight, dry, easily cooked.) Feature whole-grain flakes in your daily eating program for good taste and needed fiber. Also combine different whole-grain flakes for exciting new flavors. Mix oat flakes, rice flakes, rye flakes, triticale flakes, wheat flakes, soybean flakes in any desired combination, either two or four or six or what-have-you? The possibilities are endless adventures in high-fiber good eating.

A SELECTION OF HIGH-FIBER FOODS

BULGER OR COUSCOUS. Wheat that has been parboiled to help pop off some of the bran and crack the kernels, then dried to improve storability. Also called parboiled wheat; it is whole wheat that has been cooked, dried, partly debranned, and cracked into coarse, angular fragments. Rehydration requires simmering for 15 to 25 minutes. It may be used as an alternate for rice in many recipes. It resembles whole wheat in nutritive properties. This ancient all-wheat food originated in the Near East. Bulgur and cracked wheat (which has not been cooked) are usually interchangeable in recipes.

BROWN RICE. The whole unpolished grain of rice with only the outer inedible fibrous hull removed. In its hulled state it is a good source of bran as well as vitamins and minerals. Also known as hulled rice.

RICE CREAM. A delicious high-bran cereal made from whole long-grain brown rice. The brown rice is roasted by the dry radiant method and then stone ground a little coarser than rice flour. Good for breakfast cereals and baked goods.

WHOLE GRAINS. Available as whole-grain berries for cooking, as is, or for cereals as well as the basis for main dishes. Unprocessed whole grains offer good bran content.

GRANOLA. Basically a combination of flaked grains, seeds, nuts, and/or fruits. A typical granola cereal contains wheat, rye, and oat flakes, seedless raisins, sesame seeds, sunflower seeds, slivered almonds, and hazel nuts, pure maple syrup, soy oil, sea salt, honey. Use granola as a dry snack food, as a cereal, as a topping over desserts. Sprinkle bran over granola for double-barrelled fiber supply.

BUCKWHEAT. The triangular seed of a cereal grass used as a grain. The dark flour is ground whole-grain buckwheat and a good source of bran. NOTE: Light buckwheat flour is made from sifted flour, not unroasted buckwheat groats as is generally believed; it is lower in bran content. Use dark buckwheat for baking breads, muffins, pancakes, waffles.

CORN MEAL. Made by grinding cleaned white or yellow corn to a fineness specified by federal standards. Natural or ungerminated corn is made by slowly grinding corn kernels to medium meal consistency on buhrstones (a siliceous rock used for millstones). All the corn germ and corn flour is left, so it is a good source of bran. It is not necessary to add other flours to corn meal to prevent crumbling. Corn meal contains small amounts of vegetable fat and fiber, and not more than 15 per cent moisture. Use for baking cornbreads, spoonbreads, and other breads and muffins. It is also served as a hot cereal, long known as *mush*. The cooked mush can be chilled and then sliced, sautéed, and eaten with honey. NOTE: Avoid bolted corn meal, which has had the germ and bran removed.

HOMINY. Generally made from white corn, the hull and germ may be removed if it is refined. Select *unprocessed* hominy grits, as they are called. You may cook hominy in milk or water and serve as a vegetable. You may prepare hominy grits as a casserole with cheese to serve in place of potatoes or rice.

MILLET. A seed grain with an alkaline ash that tends to balance the ash of acid cereals. A prime source of most essential amino acids. Its protein content is said to be equal to that of animal foods. Unprocessed millet will give you a good source of bran. Use as a cereal. Its unusually high quality of millet protein and lecithin makes it an excellent meat extender. TIP: For variety, try millet in place of rice in any recipe.

OATS. A cereal grass. Oats were originally a staple food of Scotland. Today, oats are available in different forms: *Flour*—finely ground from oat groats, used to blend with other flours in baking. *Groats*—untreated, natural, hulled oats with only the chaff removed, used with other grains for a cereal. *Rolled Oats*—Flaked oats to be eaten raw or cooked; largely separate flakes. Cooks into large chewy flakes when properly steamed. Use for cereal, baked goods. *Steel-Cut*—Natural, unrefined oat groats cut into small cubes for a tasty, chewy cereal. For cereal, or for variations, blend with cracked wheat or millet. The original "porridge." Makes a delicious cereal.

RYE. A hardy annual grass that is widely cultivated as both a cereal grass and cover crop. Available in different forms: *Flour*—a finely ground product obtained by sifting rye meal. May be mixed with other whole-grain flours for baking. *Grits*—whole rye cracked into six or eight pieces, free from flour for use as a cereal or mixing with other grits or meals for adding to bread. *Meal*—Pumpernickel type rye whole ground to the consistency of coarse corn meal. Blend with other meals or flours in baking. Rye is often found in granola and unprocessed cereals. A good source of bran.

TRITICALE. A newly developed grain variety. A combination of wheat (triticum) and rye (secale). This wheat-rye combination is a prime source of bran. It is also 40 per cent higher in protein than most other grains. Improved amino acid balance provides triticale with a better protein efficiency ratio or a biological value closer to that of eggs and meat than if wheat and rye were taken separately. Very nutritious when cooked whole, sprouted, or flaked for use in cereals, casseroles, meat loaves, etc. Triticale flour makes excellent high-fiber bread but it should be mixed with other, higher gluten flours, for its own protein has little gluten. A distinctive, slightly sweet taste. Sprinkle over whole-grain cereals with bran for top-notch fiber intake.

WHOLE WHEAT. Also known as whole-grain or graham flour. The natural constituents of the wheat, which include bran, remain unaltered during the milling process. Various brands include: *Red Winter Wheat*—Hard Montana and North Dakota spring wheat grown in soils of high mineral composition where the land rebuilds through a long-range rotation plan. Has a high alkaline ash, good for breads, hard rolls, most baked goods. *Cracked Wheat*—Red wheat cracked into 4 to 6 separate pieces, free from flour. These angular fragments may be used for cereal, meat loaf, casseroles, soups, burgers, patties, etc. *Durum Wheat*—a high-gluten flour used for making semolina, which is then used for macaroni, spaghetti, and other pasta. Use whole wheat for baking and for cereals for good bran-fiber content.

WHEAT GERM. A high bran source if you use the untreated, natural embryo of select wheat. Wheat germ is the seed of the wheat and a prime bran source. Use for baking, breading, for adding to cereals.

BROWN RICE FLOUR. Stone-ground long-grain brown rice. Combine with whole-wheat flour in breads, batters, or use alone for cookies with crispness.

RYE FLOUR. Stone-ground whole-grain rye. Mix with whole-wheat flour because rye by itself tends to be heavy. Makes a delicious party and sandwich bread. Add caraway seeds for better flavor and more fiber, too.

ALFALFA SEEDS. Deep-rooted leguminous plant which may be mixed with flour for baking or sprinkled over cereals, soups, salads, and desserts.

ALMONDS. Nut-like kernel of a small tree of the peach family. Eat raw or toasted. Mix with baked goods. Excellent source of fiber. For a super treat, blanch almonds, roast them and grind into almond butter for use on a whole-grain slice of bread.

PEANUTS. Not a nut, but a legume with a high-fiber content. Eat them, as is, in the form of peanut butter; or chop, and sprinkle over cereals or add to baked goods.

PECANS, WALNUTS. Delicious nuts that are good sources of minerals as well as fiber. Eat as a snack, or chop and add to baked goods, soups, salads, casseroles, sauces.

SESAME SEEDS. Small flat seeds harvested from an East Indian annual herb plant. Add to breads, grains, vegetables. Try sesame butter, which is made of ground roasted sesame seeds. Blenderize them with water and honey for sesame milk. Or grind sesame seeds to make *tahini*, a butter used as you would any nut butter. Keep refrigerated in a tightly closed jar. Very good fiber source.

SUNFLOWER SEEDS. A plant source of unusually high fiber content. Get untreated natural sunflower seeds. Good for munching, or for sprinkling over soups, salads, casseroles, sauces, cereals.

SEVEN-GRAIN CEREAL. A high-fiber combination of seven unrefined grinds of wheat, corn, barley, oats, rye, soybeans, bran, and rice bran for use as a cooked cereal. Add raisins or dates for sweetening. Tasty as a breakfast cereal.

Also use in puddings, soups, casseroles, meat loaves and patties, and as a meat extender. Replace small amount of flour when baking.

RICE BRAN. This consists of bran and germ with varying quantities of hull. It is a smooth brownish powder with a faintly sweet taste. It is the outer bran layer removed from rice. Use moderately since it is very potent. Mix with flour for baking. Sprinkle over cereals.

RICE POLISH. The inner bran layers and some endosperm of rice. It is a smooth yellowish powder with a sweetish taste. High in bran. Add to foods as you would wheat germ.

WHOLE-GRAIN CEREALS. These retain the natural proportions of bran, germ, and endosperm and the specific nutrients that are normally contained in the whole *unprocessed* grain. Excellent source of bran and fiber. Whenever buying packaged cereals, it should be whole grain or natural and unprocessed.

BARLEY. A high-bran cereal grass. Select the natural white barley, which may have the hull removed but is *not* pearled (another name for polished) so it has good bran content. A flavorful addition to soups, casseroles, cereals.

KASHA. Another name for buckwheat groats—that is, buckwheat hulled grain broken into fragments. Use as a cereal or as a binder in breads, meat loaves, casseroles, soups. A rich, nut-like flavor.

FLAXSEED. A slender herb that is an excellent source of bran. Sprinkle over cereals. Combine with other grains for a tasty mixture.

GLUTEN FLOUR. A low-starch flour made by washing the starch from high-protein wheat flour. The gluten is dried and ground. When using gluten flour for baking, more soya, rye or other specialty flours can be used for a good flavor and higher bran content.

UNBOLTED GRAINS. You will find unbolted cornmeal (or other grains) in the store. This may be either water or stone-ground. Unbolted means that the bran and germ have not been removed, as it has been in the "degerminated" corn meal. Always select the *unbolted* grain, which is the key source of needed bran.

BLACK BEANS. A variety of soybeans. Use in thick soups, in Oriental and Mediterranean dishes. Black beans are good for any recipe, but very delicious in soup.

BLACKEYED PEAS. This is actually a bean; also called "cow peas." Small, oval-shaped, and creamy white with a black spot on one side, they are used primarily as a main-dish vegetable.

GARBANZO BEANS. Also known as chick peas, they are nut-flavored. May be used as a main-dish vegetable. Light brown in color and irregularly shaped. Use as a dip, sauce, in soups, and salads.

GREAT NORTHERN BEANS. Medium-sized, oval, and white, can be used for soups, salads, home-baked beans, most casseroles.

KIDNEY BEANS. Large, red or white in color, and kidney-shaped, very popular for salads, chili, and Mexican dishes.

LENTILS. Dark-colored and spicy flavored, they make a very filling soup; may also be added to casseroles. Good fiber source.

LIMA BEANS. Broad and flat, available in different size, but has no influence on quality. Select size you want. Use for casseroles, and vegetable dishes.

MUNG BEANS. Small green dried beans that are good as a quickly cooked vegetable or as a fresh and tangy addition to salads.

NAVY BEANS. This category includes Great Northern, pea, flat small white, and small white beans. Use for home-baked beans, soups, casseroles, in salads.

DRY PEAS. These may be green or yellow; the green type has a more distinctive flavor. Available either whole or split. Use to make soups, casseroles, vegetable side dishes, dips, and hors d'oeuvres. *Dry split peas* have had their skins removed and are mainly used for soup. Green and yellow *whole* peas and green and yellow *split* peas, even though they may vary in taste a little, are used interchangeably in many recipes.

PINTO BEANS. Brown-speckled, in the same family as kidney and red beans, they are used mainly in salads and chili.

RED and PINK BEANS. Related to the kidney bean, very good for most Mexican dishes, chili, and as a vegetable dish.

SOYBEANS. Called the "meat of the Orient." Rich in almost all known nutrients and a top-notch source of fiber. Use as a vegetable, meat extender, meat substitute.

YOUR FIBER COUNTER

Food	Grams of Fiber
Bran, 1 ounce	2.2
Bran, miller's, 1 ounce	3.1
Millet, 3½ ounces	3.2
Rye flour, dark, 3½ ounces	2.4
Soy flour, defatted, 1 cup stirred	3.2
Wheat flour, whole-wheat, ¾ cup	2.3

Apple, raw, whole, 1 medium	1.5
Apricots, dried, uncooked, 17 large halves	3.0
Blackberries, raw, 1 cup	5.9
Blueberries, raw, 1 cup	2.1
Dates, pitted, cut, 1 cup	4.1
Figs, fresh, raw, 2 large or 3 small	1.2
Kumquats, raw, 5 to 6 medium	3.7
Pears, raw, ½ pear	1.4
Raspberries, black, raw, ⅔ cup	5.1
Raspberries, red, raw, ¾ cup	3.0
Strawberries, raw, whole 10 large	1.3
Almonds, dried, unblanched, ⅔ cup	2.7
Chestnuts, fresh and shelled, ½ cup scant	1.1
Filberts or hazelnuts, 10 to 12 nuts	2.3
Peanuts, raw, with skin, 3½ ounces	4.3
Peanut butter, natural, 6 tablespoons	2.0
Pecans, shelled, no salt, 1 cup halves	2.2
Walnuts, English, 1 cup halves	2.1
Beans, common, white ½ cup scant	4.3
Beans, dry, pinto, raw, ½ cup	4.3
Chickpeas, or garbanzos, ½ cup	5.0
Cow peas, ½ cup	4.4
Lentils, ½ cup	3.9
Peas, common, ½ cup	4.9
Pumpkin and squash kernels, 3½ ounces	1.9
Sesame seeds, 3½ ounces	2.4
Soybeans, ½ cup	4.9
Sunflower seed kernels	3.8

HOW TO GET MORE VALUE FOR YOUR BRAN-FIBER SHOPPING DOLLAR

When selecting high-fiber foods, you can get more value for your shopping dollar with these little-known but highly important suggestions and tips:

1. Buckwheat flour should be used for baking as much as possible. The reason is in the unique way that the flour is made from this cereal grass-herb. The seeds of buck-

wheat are first ground then sifted through a coarse bolting cloth. Particles of the hull pass through the cloth, giving the flour its characteristic dark color and flavor. As used, buckwheat flour is a mixture of the high-fiber ground seeds together with wheat flour. The latter modifies the naturally strong flavor of the buckwheat. Because the flour itself is not sifted, the germ is retained. This germ is a very concentrated source of needed bran and will give you a high fiber intake.

2. Bran should be used as a filler or binder for many main dishes and, of course, as part of your cereals. Bran is the leader in high-fiber food count. It is made from the ground husks of wheat, rye, corn, and other grains separated from the flour. The nutritive value of these husks increases as the miller removes heavier and heavier coats from the grain. The inner skins, called *pollards,* are the most choice. Unprocessed bran will have *pollards* that provide you with much needed fiber.

3. Rice should be brown. No other type of rice should be used since the husks and bran have been removed. White rice has been polished and debranded as well as chemicalized so it would be unsuitable for optimum health purposes. So-called "converted" or "parboiled" rice has been precooked and dried before polishing. The converting process forces much of the vitamin B into the grain before the bran is removed. While this conserves some of the original nutrients, it destroys its bran. So white rice should be avoided by the fiber seeker, and brown rice should be used frequently.

4. Health stores and supermarkets offer cracked wheat, which is made from the toasted grain and with the bran and germ intact. This is a tasty source of bran and fiber. Prepare cracked wheat in the same manner as you do brown rice. It flatters meat and vegetable dishes. Good with fish, too.

5. Enjoy kasha, or buckwheat groats. Kasha is actually the fruit of the buckwheat plant and a prime source of bran. In some homes cooked kasha with bow noodles,

known as *kasha varnishkas,* serve as a delicious accompaniment to many meals. Delicious!

6. Flour gives you good fiber. But you should use the nutritious kind that is labeled *unbleached*. Pass up any flours that state they are "bromated" or "phosphated." (Government laws require these processes to be stated on the label.) Instead, select any unbleached or whole-grain flour for good bran-creating fiber.

7. Instead of cornstarch, you could use arrowroot powder, which is made from the arrowroot plant and a good source of bran. But if you do use cornstarch, remember that this is a finely milled starch obtained from corn by removing the bran and grinding the remaining kernels. Without the bran, cornstarch will not give you needed fiber. But cornstarch is not usually treated with chemicals to alter its color or cooking properties. So you may want to use it as a thickening agent for sauces or desserts. But it is not to be considered a good bran source.

8. Oats are high on the list of good bran-fiber foods. Oatmeal is also a good food. When oats are milled, the bran and germ remain in the edible portion. Try any old-fashioned type of oatmeal for good fiber. Steel-cut oats may require a bit longer cooking time but are high in bran and fiber. Further enrich the value of the oatmeal by cooking in milk, instead of water. While many of the quick-cooking oats may not have additives, they have been very processed and the bran content reduced. Take a few more moments in cooking for greater bran value.

9. Corn meal is a good source of bran. Be sure that the corn meal says it is "unbolted" and/or "undegerminated" since this means the bran has not been removed. Otherwise, "bolted" or "pearled" or "germinated" corn meal will give you bran-deficient grains. Degerminated corn meal has also been synthetically enriched so it is chemicalized and not recommended. Yellow corn meal is higher in vitamin A than white. Use corn meal as a high bran food in place of

farina, cream of wheat, cream of white, all of which have had their bran and germ removed. Stone- or water-ground yellow corn meal is the best for your bran-fiber content.

10. For a delicious treat try any of the Swiss breakfast cereals available in health stores and supermarkets. Also known as *muesli,* these cereals combine oat flakes, dried apple flakes, wheat and rye, millet flakes, raisins, unrefined sugar, crushed almonds, wheat germ, and honey. There may be some variations in the ingredients but all of these Swiss-style cereals are natural prime sources of needed fiber. Add milk to this cereal and enjoy a soft, rich porridge that is naturally sweet, high in bran, and very satisfying. You can add a spoon of bran for even more fiber. It's the tasty way to build good health.

Once you plan to use fiber foods in your diet, you will discover one adventure after another in good eating—and better health.

ALL ABOUT BRAN—IN A NUTSHELL

Bran, in addition to being a good source of nutrients, also is a rich source of *food fiber* (known as bulk or roughage). This food fiber takes the wastes that are left behind by the digestive processes. Instead of letting them wait in the system, food fiber hurries them through to be eliminated. Bran does more than establish regularity. *Bran shortens the time that the wastes are stored.*

Dietary fiber itself is made up of complex carbohydrates (such as pectin and cellulose) and other substances that enter into the construction of the cell walls and structural components of plants.

How Bran Works. Bran fiber stimulates the normal action of the intestinal tract during the processes of digestion, absorption and elimination. Bran fiber provides bulk, partially, by absorbing many times its weight in liquid, producing a softer intestinal food mass. The greater bulk promotes regularity and more frequent elimination.

More Sources of Fiber. Variety is important because dietary fiber consists of many substances; the composition differs in cereals, fruits, vegetables, seeds, nuts. You should aim for a variety of food fiber from bran, whole-grain flour, and cereals, potatoes, fresh fruits and vegetables, dried beans and peas. NOTE: Breads and breakfast cereals made from *whole wheat* contain more fiber than products made from wheat from which the bran has been removed.

Most raw fruits (such as apples) contain roughage in the skins, not present in processed products. Seed fruits (strawberries, raspberries, figs) are high in fiber. You will also find fiber in most raw and cooked vegetables.

A good rule of thumb is to use *unrefined, nonprocessed* foods that have more roughage than refined foods. The refining-processing methods remove much of the fiber.

Miracle Health Power of Fiber. Whether from bran or other foods, fiber has a miracle healing power. Fiber is not digested in the intestinal tract because the human digestive system has no enzymes that can break down fiber completely. The chief value of fiber is in its ability to take up water and swell when it gets to the colon. This makes your stools soft and large; *fiber sweeps the colon clean and does it quickly.*

Doctors say that a fast transit time of waste matter is the key to protection against illness. There is difficulty when impacted fecal or waste matter jams against the wall of the colon. It irritates the mucosa which serves to protect the colon from harm. The longer the fecal matter stays there, the more fats can break through the protective mucosa and cause cancer of the colon. Also, the bad bacteria, which multiply fast when the fecal matter moves so slowly, cause diverticulosis because of pressure in the colon.

Colon Trouble. Most of the trouble comes in the sigmoid colon (just before the rectum; it gets its name because it is shaped like the letter S.) The sigmoid slows the waste matter down so a lot of it won't get into the rectum at one time and cause too-frequent bowel movements. But when it becomes impacted, trouble starts.

At the point where blood vessels enter and leave the sigmoid, there are no muscles. At those weak spots, the mucous membrane is pushed out by gas, much like a flying wedge by gas, forming a diverticulum. The point of the wedge pushes through the bowel wall. After the wall is pierced, pressure makes the sac bulge into a globe connected to the inside of the bowel. When the ailment worsens, the muscle layer thickens at the bottom near the colon wall and forms a narrow neck like a grape on a stem.

The "grapes" fill up with waste matter. But they cannot expel the waste since the upper part has no muscle. Wastes that remain in the "grapes" eventually block the diverticula. Behind the plug, an assortment of unhealthy bacteria develops. This can lead to adhesions to nearby viscera, peritonitis, abscesses, and fistula. Chronic diverticulitis is inflammation of the peritoneum (the membrane lining the body cavity).

These are problems that are caused by accumulated wastes. Doctors feel that a balanced diet with adequate fiber can help maintain regularity and reasonable protection against such life-destroying responses.

A high-fiber diet along with natural and nonprocessed foods can help cleanse your internal organs and protect you against the risk of ill health.

PART II

YOUR BRAN-FIBER COOKBOOK

CHAPTER 8

BRAN BEVERAGES

BRAN COFFEE

⅔ cup undeterminated corn meal
2 cups bran
½ cup boiling water
⅓ cup molasses

Mix dry ingredients. Add boiling water to molasses and mix well. Pour this over the grain and stir until thoroughly mixed. Turn into a shallow baking pan. Bake at 375°F., stirring several times until color is uniform and almost black. Do not let burn. Remove. Store in a tightly covered jar.

FLAXSEED TEA

¼ cup flaxseed
3 cups boiling water
2 tablespoons lemon juice

Put flaxseed into boiling water. Boil gently for 2 hours. Drain, season liquid with lemon juice. Honey may be added for flavoring. More lemon juice may be added if desired.

HEALTH COCKTAIL

1 glass pineapple juice
4 young tender dandelion leaves
4 lettuce leaves
6 pitted dates
2 sprigs parsley

Liquefy in a blender and serve promptly.

NOTE: When making any kind of green drink, use raw greens for good fiber content. You may use chives, dandelions, all varieties of lettuce, beet tops, collards, spinach, chard, kale, turnip tops, watercress, green peppers, tender asparagus.

MORNING SHAKE

¾ cup milk
⅓ cup tomato juice
¼ cup wheat germ

Put all ingredients into a blender jar or small bowl. Blend at high speed with a blender, mixer, or rotary beater. Serve promptly.

COFFEE NOG

2 cups cold milk
⅛ teaspoon vanilla
1 egg
2 tablespoons wheat germ
2 tablespoons honey
2 teaspoons cereal coffee such as Postum

Put all ingredients into a blender jar or small bowl. Blend at high speed. Serve promptly.

BEAUTY FRAPPÉ

¾ cup skimmed milk
¼ cup orange (or any flavor) sherbet
2 tablespoons wheat germ

Combine all ingredients in a blender jar or small bowl.
Blend at high speed. Serve cold.

LUNCHEON SHAKE

¾ cup chilled buttermilk
3 tablespoons wheat germ

Combine in a blender or small bowl. Whizz or thoroughly
combine. Makes an excellent luncheon beverage.

BRAN BROTH

1 cup bran
2 cups cold water
1 cup hot water

Soak bran in water overnight. Next morning pour into
strainer and drain. Pour 1 cup hot water through the bran,
stirring thoroughly, rinsing as much as possible. Drink
slowly.

ALFALFA BEVERAGE

1 cup alfalfa seed
2 quarts cold water

Bring seed and water to a boil. Cool, strain, store in glass
jar in refrigerator. Use ¼ to ½ glass of this extract, fill
glass with water. Serve either piping hot or refreshingly

cold. Honey is optional. Add mint leaves for a delightful change.

RICE POLISH COCKTAIL

1 cup milk (whole or skim)
2 tablespoons rice polish
1 tablespoon honey or desired sweetening
4 or 5 drops vanilla
1 tablespoon powdered skim milk
1 teaspoon carob powder (at health stores)

Pour one-half of the milk into a blender. Add all remaining ingredients. Mix thoroughly. Now add remaining one-half cup of milk. Mix a few seconds longer.

CRANBERRY JUICE COCKTAIL

2 cups raw cranberries
3 cups water
½ cup honey
2 tablespoons lemon juice

Wash cranberries and cook in water in covered kettle about 5 minutes, or until skins pop open. Strain through cheese-cloth. Boil cranberry juice and honey for 2 minutes, stirring until thoroughly dissolved. Add lemon juice and chill thoroughly. Serve in small cocktail glasses.

TOMATO CREAM COCKTAIL

1 cup chilled cream
2 cups chilled tomato juice
4 grated celery stalks
¼ cup crushed ice
Pinch of salt
Dash of cayenne
Drop of Tabasco

Combine all ingredients in shaker or glass jar, using very small amounts of seasonings. Shake vigorously and pour over additional crushed ice.

BERRY PUNCH

    1 pint seasonal berries (cranberries are good)
    1 pint water
    1 cup skim milk
    ½ cup orange juice
    1½ tablespoons lemon juice
    1 pint seltzer

Wash cranberries and cook in water in covered kettle until cranberries are mushy. Strain through cheesecloth and cool. Add milk, orange juice, and lemon juice. Add seltzer last. Pour over block of clear ice in punch bowl.

RASPBERRY MILK SHAKE

    ¾ cup fresh raspberries
    1¼ cups milk
    1 cup yoghurt
    Few whole raspberries

Wash berries, drain well, and crush with a potato masher. Measure and combine with milk and three-fourths of the yoghurt. Shake or beat until mixture is a smooth blend. Pour into 4 glasses and top each with remaining yoghurt and 1 or 2 whole raspberries. Serve promptly.

HOT ALMOND EGGNOG

6 eggs, separated
¼ cup honey
6 cups milk, scalded
1 tablespoon almond flavoring
1 tablespoon vanilla
⅓ cup yoghurt
Few grains grated nutmeg
4 tablespoons almonds and other nuts, slivered

Beat egg whites stiff and save. Set aside. Beat yolks until light, add honey and blend. Add hot milk and flavorings. Fold egg whites into mixture. Pour into cups and top with yoghurt. Sprinkle with nutmeg and almonds.

DATE DRINK

1 cup chopped sun-dried dates
2 cups fruit juice
1 egg

Blend all ingredients until smooth. Serve chilled.

BRAN-NUT MILK SHAKE

1 tall glass milk
2 tablespoons bran
1 teaspoon blackstrap or unsulphured molasses
2 tablespoons chopped or ground almonds

Mix all ingredients together thoroughly. Serve chilled.

MIDDAY PICKUP

1 cup milk
2 tablespoons rice polishings
1 tablespoon honey
½ teaspoon vanilla
1 tablespoon powdered milk
1 teaspoon carob powder (at health stores)

Mix all ingredients with ½ cup of the milk. Blend until thoroughly combined. Now add remaining milk. Mix a few seconds more.

GREEN FIBER DRINK

6 large almonds, with skins on
1 teaspoon sunflower seeds
1 teaspoon bran
1 teaspoon oats
1 teaspoon rye
1 teaspoon barley
1 teaspoon millet
1 teaspoon sesame seeds
1 teaspoon flax seeds
1 cup water
1 cup any fruit juice
Sun-dried fruits
Few sprigs parsley

NOTE: Begin by soaking all dry ingredients overnight in the cup of water.

Next morning, blenderize 3 minutes. Add 1 cup any desired fruit juice. Now add sun-dried fruits such as raisins, pitted dates, and add sprigs of parsley and other greens. Liquefy 5 seconds longer. Drink at room temperature.

TROPICAL FIBER DRINK

1 peeled grapefruit with white membrane
1 peeled orange with white membrane
4 tablespoons honey
1 peeled lemon with white membrane
½ cup papaya pulp
1 cup water or fruit juice

Combine all ingredients and liquefy in blender. Chill. May be refrigerated until ready for use.

EMERALD COCKTAIL

1 cup grapefruit or pineapple juice
2 tablespoons parsley
Green lettuce leaves
Watercress leaves
Celery leaves

Combine all ingredients and liquefy in blender. Chill. Serve fresh.

ROSY CHEEKS COCKTAIL

3 raw beets, washed
1 cup tomato juice
1 tablespoon yoghurt
2 tablespoons minced parsley

In blender, liquefy beets. Add tomato juice. Heat slightly and serve with a yoghurt-parsley garnish.

PEANUT PUNCH

4 cups water
1 cup peanuts
2 tablespoons unsulphured molasses
2 tablespoons brewer's yeast

Blend all ingredients together. Drink chilled.

NUT MILK

4 cups water
1 cup cashews or other assorted nuts
5 dates

Blend all ingredients together. Drink chilled.

MILK-BRAN SHAKE

4 cups milk
3 tablespoons bran
2 tablespoons unsulphured molasses
2 tablespoons brewer's yeast
¼ cup almonds, blanched

Blend all ingredients together. Drink chilled.

MILK SMOOTHIE

4 cups milk
½ cup skim milk powder
2 tablespoons brewer's yeast
2 tablespoons bran
1 tablespoon unsulphured molasses
1 tablespoon honey

Blend all ingredients together. Drink chilled.

CHAPTER 9

BREAKFAST SPECIALS

FRUIT-BRAN DELIGHT

Bake thick apple wedges until tender with honey to sweeten, a dash of cinnamon, cloves, a dot of butter, and thin slices of lemon. Top a bowl of whole bran flakes with apple wedges. Serve with milk, cream, or yoghurt. Serves 1.

BERRY HALF-AND-HALF

Pile strawberries, blackberries, raspberries, or blueberries (or mixtures) on one side of a cereal dish and whole bran flakes on the other side. Sprinkle honey between the two. Serve with milk. Serves 1.

CHEESE-BRAN BREAKFAST

In the center of a bowl with adequate whole bran flakes, place a mound of cottage cheese. Garnish with fruit slices and/or chopped nuts. Serve with milk. Serves 1.

PEAR-BRAN BREAKFAST

Bake pear halves until tender with honey to sweeten, a dot of butter, and a small wedge of orange on each. Top a bowl of whole bran flakes with slices of baked pear. Serve with milk or cream. Serves 1.

BRANCAKES WITH CITRUS SYRUP

1 cup light corn syrup
⅓ cup orange juice
2 tablespoons grated orange peel (optional)
1½ cups sifted regular whole-wheat flour
3 teaspoons baking powder
1 egg
2 tablespoons honey
2 cups milk
½ cup whole bran flakes

To Prepare Citrus Syrup: measure corn syrup and orange juice into small saucepan; bring to boil. Remove from heat; stir in 1 tablespoon of the orange peel. Serve warm or cooled over Brancakes.

To Make Brancakes: sift together flour and baking powder. Set aside. In large mixing bowl beat egg until foamy. Stir in honey, milk, the remaining 1 tablespoon of the orange peel, and the whole bran flakes. Let stand 1 to 2 minutes or until cereal is softened. Add sifted dry ingredients, stirring to combine. Batter will be lumpy. Now dip up batter, using ¼ cup dry measure; cook on oiled and pre-heated griddle, turning once, until well-browned on both sides. Serve hot with Citrus Syrup. Yield: 14 pancakes, about 5 inches in diameter.

CORN MEAL MUSH

1 cup undegerminated corn meal (yellow or white)
½ cup cold water
4 cups milk, whole or skimmed

Stir meal into ½ cup cold water. Heat milk to boiling, add moistened meal. Mix well. When thickened, place in top of double boiler or over very low even heat and cook for about 30 to 45 minutes depending on the flavor desired.

Serve hot with butter or milk or pour into loaf pan to cool. (TIP: To use cold leftover mush, coat with bran, sauté in oil, and serve hot with honey.) Serves 2.

MILLET CEREAL

1 cup water
1 cup milk
½ cup millet
1 tablespoon honey
Sun-dried raisins

Bring water and milk to boil in top part of double boiler (direct heat). Add millet. Boil 5 minutes, then steam over boiling water for 30 minutes. Add honey and raisins and steam 5 minutes longer. Serves 4 to 6.

BREAKFAST CREAMY KERNELS

½ cup buckwheat groats (kasha)
2½ cups water
2 tablespoons honey
Milk or cream

Combine buckwheat groats and water in medium-sized saucepan. Bring to a boil. Cook over low heat 10 minutes, stirring occasionally. Stir in honey. Serve with milk or cream and more honey. Makes about 2 cups.

BOILED BULGUR

2 cups water
1 cup bulgur (couscous)

Heat water to boiling. Stir bulgur into boiling water. Cover tightly and cook over very low heat 20 minutes. Do not remove while cooking. Serves 6, ½ cup each.

OVEN-COOKED BULGUR

1 cup bulgur (couscous)
2 cups boiling water

Preheat oven to 350°F. (moderate). Place bulgur in a 1-quart casserole. Pour boiling water over bulgur, stir and cover. Bake 25 minutes or until tender. Serves 6, ½ cup each. SUGGESTION: For added flavor, cook bulgur in beef or chicken broth. Or add two beef or chicken bouillon cubes to the water in which bulgur is cooked.

BASIC HOMINY GRITS

5 cups water
1 cup hominy grits

Bring water to boil. Stir in hominy grits slowly. Lower heat and stir until thickened. Cook for 15 minutes longer, stirring occasionally to keep from sticking. Serves 8, ½ cup each.

OATMEAL-PRUNE WHIP

1 cup cooked sun-dried prunes, drained and pitted
¾ cup cooked oatmeal, cooled
¼ teaspoon cinnamon
2 egg whites
¼ cup honey

Mash prunes; stir in oatmeal and cinnamon; set aside. Beat egg whites until frothy. Gradually add honey, a tablespoon at a time, beating constant until stiff and glossy. Gently fold in prune mixture. Spoon into 6 individual dishes or large serving dish. Chill several hours or until set. Serves 6.

CROWN OATMEAL

2 cups oats, uncooked
4 cups water

FLAKY OATMEAL: Stir oats into briskly boiling water. Cook until mushy. Cover pan, remove from heat and let stand a few minutes before serving.

CREAMY OATMEAL: Put oats and cold water in pan. Bring to a boil. Cover pan. Remove from heat and let stand a few minutes before serving.

FRUIT-BLENDED OATMEAL: Add ½ cup chopped pitted dates, chopped prunes, raisins, dried apricots, or chopped apple to the water just before stirring in the oats. Bring to a boil. Cover pan. Remove from heat and let stand a few minutes before serving.

CROWNS FOR OATMEAL: Top each serving with a dollop of honey, your favorite preserves, fruit slices, applesauce, dates, raisins, maple-blended syrup, or sliced bananas. Serves 6.

OATMEAL-BUTTERMILK PANCAKES

2 cups oats, uncooked
½ teaspoon baking soda
2½ cups buttermilk
1 cup buckwheat flour
2 teaspoons baking powder
1 tablespoon honey
⅓ cup melted or liquid shortening
2 eggs, beaten

Add oats and soda to buttermilk. Let stand 5 minutes. Sift together flour and baking powder. Add sifted dry ingredients, honey, shortening, and eggs to oats mixture. Stir until combined. For each pancake, pour about ¼ cup batter onto hot, lightly oiled griddle. Bake to a golden brown, turning only once. Serve hot with butter and maple syrup. Makes 14 to 16 pancakes.

OATMEAL COOKED IN MILK

2 cups milk
2 cups water
2 cups oats, uncooked

Combine milk and water in saucepan. Bring to a boil. Stir in oats and cook from 3 to 5 minutes, stirring occasionally. Cover pan, remove from heat and let stand a few minutes before serving. Serves 6.

CRISP OATMEAL SLICES

2 cups oats, uncooked
3½ cups boiling water
½ cup finely chopped nuts, seeds

Stir oats into briskly boiling water. Cook from 3 to 5 minutes. Cover pan. Remove from heat. Let stand 5 minutes. Stir in nuts and seeds. Pour into unoiled loaf pan. Cool slightly. Cover and refrigerate several hours or overnight. Cut into 16 slices. Sauté in small amount of oil or butter until golden brown, about 10 minutes per side. Serve hot with butter and maple syrup. Serves 8.

CREAMED BREAKFAST RICE

2 cups cooked brown rice
¾ cup sun-dried raisins
1½ cups milk

Mix ingredients. Pour into deep casserole dish. Cover. Bake for 45 minutes at 325°F. Do not let milk boil or it will curdle. Serves 2.

SWEDISH RYE MUSH

⅔ cup unbleached rye flour
3 cups lukewarm water
½ cup sun-dried fruit slices

Beat the rye flour into the lukewarm water so it is free of lumps. Now cook over a high flame but continue to stir rapidly. When it starts to boil, turn heat to low, and cook for 10 minutes, stirring occasionally. Add fruit slices just before taking from the stove. This mush thickens even after removing from stove. Serves 4.

ROLLED OAT AND SEED CEREAL

1 cup rolled oats
½ cup ground sunflower seeds
3 cups boiling water

Mix oats and sunflower seeds together and stir into boiling water. Cover. Turn heat to low and cook for 5 minutes. Serves 4.

STEAMED WHOLE WHEAT KERNELS

1 cup wheat germ
5 cups hot water

Combine wheat germ with water. Let boil for 30 minutes. Then set in a double boiler, cooking until thoroughly done. Serves 4 to 6.

MIXED-GRAIN CEREAL

2 cups soy grits
2 cups rye grits

2 cups steel-cut oats
2 cups cracked whole wheat

Mix all grains together in a jar and keep in refrigerator. When ready to cook, use 1 cup mixed grain to 4 cups boiling water. Serves 2 to 4.

CRACKED WHEAT CEREAL

1 cup cracked wheat
4 cups boiling water

Soak wheat in water overnight. Next morning, boil in the 4 cups of water until soft. Serves 4. (This may be cooked the night before and warmed in double boiler for breakfast.)

STEAMED MILLET

3 cups water
1 cup milk
1 cup millet
1 tablespoon honey
½ cup dates, chopped fine (or 1 cup raisins)

Heat water and milk to lukewarm. Add millet and other ingredients and bring to boil. Put in casserole. Steam for 1 hour or until soft and about twice the volume. Serves 2.

SPROUTED WHEAT-OATMEAL CEREAL

1¼ cups oatmeal
4 cups boiling water
1 cup sprouted wheat (at health stores)

Stir oatmeal into boiling water. Add sprouted wheat gradually. Cook over low heat for 20 minutes. Serves 4.

HOMEMADE GRANOLA

3 cups whole wheat flour
2 cups undegerminated corn meal
1 cup wheat germ
3 cups dried coconut
6 cups rolled oats
1 cup vegetable oil
1 cup honey
1 to 2 cups water

Mix dry ingredients. Add oil, honey, then water a little at a time. Mix until crumbly. Bake in a slow oven, about 250°F., stirring every 15 minutes or so until thoroughly dry and light brown. This will keep well. Use as a homemade granola, with milk, as desired.

BARLEY CEREAL

1 cup cracked whole barley
5 cups water
1 cup chopped dates, figs or prunes (or mixtures)

Soak barley overnight in the water. Next morning, cook in the same water until soft, about 20 minutes. Add chopped fruit. Serves 4.

CORN MEAL PORRIDGE

2 cups yellow or undegerminated corn meal
3 cups combination of milk and water

Boil liquid. When bubbly, mix in the corn meal slowly to keep it free from lumps. Stir gently. When mixed thoroughly, cook covered for 5 minutes. Serves 6.

BREAKFAST FRUIT-WHEAT DELIGHT

1 cup sun-dried apricots
2 cups water
1 cup cracked whole wheat

Soak the apricots overnight in the water. Next morning, add cracked whole wheat and cook for 20 minutes over low flame. Serves 4.

TRY ADDING TO YOUR COOKED
OR DRY CEREALS:

- Grated apple
- Sliced fresh peaches
- Grated coconut
- Wheat germ
- Ground nuts—pecans, walnuts, peanuts, almonds or hazelnuts
- Fresh raspberries, blueberries, huckleberries, strawberries, blackberries, and boysenberries, or cooked cranberries
- Brewer's yeast
- Ripe persimmons
- Sliced guavas, bananas, or papayas
- Chopped dates, figs, raisins
- Unprocessed bran

CHAPTER 10

BREADS, ROLLS, MUFFINS

WHOLE WHEAT-BRAN YEAST BREAD

1 cup regular all-purpose unbleached flour
1 cup whole wheat flour
1 cup whole bran cereal
1 tablespoon honey
1 teaspoon salt
1 package active dry yeast
¾ cup milk
1 tablespoon unsulphured molasses
3 tablespoons margarine or butter
1 egg
Melted margarine or butter

1. In small mixing bowl stir together regular all-purpose unbleached flour and whole wheat flour. In large bowl of electric mixer, combine ½ cup of the flour mixture, the bran cereal, honey, salt, and yeast.

2. In small saucepan combine the milk, molasses, and margarine. Place over low heat until very warm (120° to 130°F.). Gradually add to cereal mixture and beat at medium speed on electric mixer for 2 minutes, scraping bowl occasionally.

3. Add egg and ¼ cup of the flour mixture. Beat at high speed on electric mixer for 2 minutes. With spoon stir in remaining flour mixture to make a stiff dough. Turn dough out onto lightly floured surface and knead 5 to 10 minutes or until smooth and elastic. Place in well-

120

oiled bowl, turning to oil top of dough. Cover with a clean cloth and let rise in warm place about 1 hour or until doubled in bulk.

4. Punch down dough. Form into smooth round ball with hands, being careful not to create large folds in dough. Place on oiled baking sheet. Cover and let rise in warm place about 1 hour or until doubled in bulk.

5. Bake on center rack of oven at 375°F. about 30 minutes or until golden brown. Remove immediately from baking sheet. Place on wire rack. Brush with melted margarine. Cool. Yield: 1 loaf.

MOLASSES BROWN BREAD

1 cup sifted regular all-purpose unbleached flour
1 teaspoon baking soda
½ teaspoon salt
½ teaspoon cinnamon (optional)
1 egg
1 cup whole-bran cereal
½ cup seedless raisins
2 tablespoons shortening
½ cup unsulphured molasses
¾ cup very hot water

1. Sift together flour, baking soda, salt, and cinnamon. Set aside.

2. In large mixing bowl beat egg until foamy. Mix in whole-bran cereal, raisins, shortening, and molasses. Add water, stirring until shortening is melted. Add sifted dry ingredients, mixing *only until combined.*

3. Fill 2 oiled metal cans, 4½ inches deep and 2¾ inches across, about ⅔ full *or* spread batter evenly in 1 oiled 9 x 5 x 3-inch loaf pan.

4. Bake in moderate oven (350°F.) about 45 minutes for bread in cans or about 35 minutes for loaf bread. Bread

is done when wooden pick inserted near center comes out clean. Remove from cans or pan; slice and serve hot. Yield: 2 loaves, 3½ x 2¾ inches, or 1 loaf, 9 x 5 inches.

LEMON-BRAN BREAD

4 eggs
1 cup water
½ cup vegetable oil
1 cup whole-bran cereal
1 18½ ounce package lemon cake mix
1 3¾ ounce package instant lemon pudding mix
½ cup sifted regular all-purpose unbleached flour
2 tablespoons poppy seeds

1. In large mixing bowl beat eggs until foamy. Add water and oil; mix well. Add remaining ingredients, mixing until all ingredients are moistened. Beat 2 minutes at medium speed of electric mixer or 400 strokes by hand. Spread batter evenly in 2 oiled 9 x 5 x 3-inch loaf pans.

2. Bake in moderate oven (350°F.) about 40 minutes or until wooden pick inserted near center comes out clean. Remove from pans. Cool completely on wire rack before slicing. Yield: 2 loaves.

BRAN BISCUITS

1½ cups sifted regular all-purpose unbleached flour
2½ teaspoons baking powder
¾ teaspoon salt
⅓ cup soft shortening
½ cup whole-bran cereal
¾ cup milk

1. Sift together flour, baking powder, and salt; place in large mixing bowl. Cut in shortening until mixture resembles coarse corn meal. Set aside.

2. Measure whole-bran cereal and milk into small mixing bowl; stir to combine. Let stand 1 to 2 minutes or until most of liquid is absorbed. Add to flour/shortening mixture, stirring *only until combined.*

3. Turn dough onto lightly floured surface; knead gently a few times. Evenly pat or roll out to about ½-inch thickness. Cut out biscuit with floured 1¾-inch biscuit cutter; place on ungreased baking sheet.

4. Bake in hot oven (425°F.) about 10 minutes or until golden brown. Serve immediately. Yield: 12 to 16 biscuits.

VARIATIONS: Split hot biscuits and top with creamed chicken to make Chicken à la King. Or place unbaked biscuits on top of your favorite creamed meat or poultry casserole for last 10 minutes of baking time, increasing oven temperature to hot (425°F.)

BRANANA-NUT BREAD

1½ cups sifted regular all-purpose unbleached flour
2 teaspoons baking powder
½ teaspoon baking soda
½ teaspoon salt
¼ cup soft shortening
⅓ cup honey
1 egg
1 teaspoon vanilla flavoring
1½ cups mashed fully ripe bananas (should have brown-flecked skins)
1 cup whole-bran cereal
½ cup coarsely chopped nuts

1. Sift together flour, baking powder, soda, and salt. Set aside.

2. Measure shortening and honey into large mixing bowl; beat until light and fluffy. Add egg and vanilla; beat well. Mix in bananas, bran, and nuts. Add sifted dry in-

gredients, mixing *only until combined*. Spread batter evenly in oiled 9 x 5 x 3-inch loaf pan.

3. Bake in moderate oven (350°F.) about 50 minutes or until wooden pick inserted near center comes out clean. Let cool 10 minutes before removing from pan. Cool completely on wire rack before slicing. Yield: 1 loaf.

BETTER BRAN MUFFINS

1¼ cups sifted regular all-purpose unbleached flour
3 teaspoons baking powder
½ teaspoon salt
1 cup whole-bran cereal
1 cup milk
1 egg
¼ cup honey
¼ cup vegetable oil or soft shortening

1. Sift together flour, baking powder and salt. Set aside.

2. Place bran and milk in mixing bowl; stir to combine. Let stand 1 to 2 minutes or until most of liquid is absorbed. Add egg, honey, and oil; beat well.

3. Add sifted dry ingredients, stirring *only until combined*. Portion batter evenly into 12 oiled 2½-inch muffin-pan cups.

4. Bake in moderately hot oven (400°F.) about 25 minutes or until muffins are golden brown. Serve immediately. Yield: 12 muffins.

GOLDEN FRUIT BREAD

1½ cups whole-bran cereal
¼ cup honey
1 cup finely cut sun-dried fruits
1½ cups boiling water

1½ cups sifted regular all-purpose unbleached flour
3 teaspoons baking powder
1 teaspoon salt
2 eggs
⅓ cup vegetable oil
Additional honey

1. Measure bran, honey, and fruit into mixing bowl. Pour boiling water over mixture; let stand until most of moisture is absorbed.

2. Sift together flour, baking powder, and salt; set aside.

3. Add eggs and vegetable oil to bran mixture. Beat well. Add flour mixture, stirring *only until combined*. Spread in lightly oiled 9 x 5 x 3-inch loaf pan. Sprinkle top with additional honey.

4. Bake in moderate oven (350°F.) about 55 minutes or until bread pulls away slightly from sides of pan. Cool thoroughly before slicing. Yield: 1 loaf.

BRAN BREAD WITH RAISINS

1½ cups sifted regular all-purpose unbleached flour
1 teaspoon baking powder
1 teaspoon baking soda
1 teaspoon salt
1½ cups whole bran cereal
1½ cups seedless raisins
¼ cup honey
¼ cup soft shortening
1½ cups hot water
1 egg
1 teaspoon vanilla flavoring
¾ cup chopped nuts

1. Sift together flour, baking powder, soda, and salt. Set aside.

2. Measure bran, raisins, honey, shortening, and hot water into mixing bowl; stir until shortening is melted. Add eggs and vanilla; beat well.

3. Add sifted dry ingredients and nuts; stir *only until combined*. Spread evenly in well-oiled 9 x 5 x 3-inch loaf pan.

4. Bake in moderate oven (350°F.) about 1 hour or until done. Cool thoroughly before slicing. Yield: 1 loaf.

HIGH-BRAN MUFFINS

1 cup whole-bran cereal
1 cup milk
1 egg
¼ cup honey
¼ cup soft shortening
1 cup sifted regular all-purpose unbleached flour
3 teaspoons baking powder
½ teaspoon salt

1. Combine bran, milk, egg, honey, and shortening in mixing bowl; beat well. Set aside.

2. Sift together flour, baking powder, and salt. Add to bran mixture, stirring *only until combined*. Fill oiled 2½-inch muffin-pan cups ¾ full.

3. Bake in moderately hot oven (400°F.) about 25 minutes. Makes 9 muffins.

SURPRISE MUFFINS

1½ cups sifted regular all-purpose unbleached flour
3 teaspoons baking powder
1 teaspoon salt

1 egg
⅔ cup milk
⅓ cup honey
⅓ cup soft shortening
1 cup whole-bran cereal
½ cup coarsely chopped nuts
¼ cup strawberry preserves
Whipped cream cheese

1. Sift together flour, baking powder, and salt. Set aside.

2. Combine egg, milk, honey, and shortening in mixing bowl; beat well. Add sifted dry ingredients, bran, and nuts, stirring *only until combined*. Fill oiled 2½-inch muffin-pan cups ⅔ full. Press a teaspoonful of strawberry preserves into the top of each muffin.

3. Bake in moderately hot oven (400°F.) about 20 minutes or until lightly browned. Top each muffin with whipped cream cheese. Serve hot. Makes 12 muffins.

BRAN-FLAVORED YEAST ROLLS

1 cup soft shortening
½ cup honey
2 cups whole-bran cereal
2 teaspoons salt
1 cup boiling water
2 packages active dry yeast
1 cup warm water (110°–115°F.)
6½ cups sifted regular all-purpose unbleached flour
2 eggs, well beaten

1. Measure shortening, honey, bran, and salt into large mixing bowl. Add boiling water; stir until shortening is melted. Let stand until lukewarm.

2. Dissolve yeast in warm water in small bowl. Set aside.

3. Add ½ of the flour to the bran mixture; mix well. Stir in dissolved yeast mixture and eggs; mix well. Add remaining flour; stir until combined. Cover bowl tightly and place in refrigerator overnight.

4. Remove dough from refrigerator 1 hour before shaping rolls. Then punch dough down and shape into small balls. Place 3 balls in each cup of an oiled 2½-inch muffin-pan; cups should be about ½ full. Let rise in warm place (85°F.) about 1 hour or until doubled in bulk.

5. Bake in hot oven (425°F.) about 12 minutes or until browned. Yield: 3 dozen rolls. NOTE: Dough may be stored in refrigerator a few days and small batches of rolls baked as needed.

CRUNCHY RAISIN MUFFINS

¼ cup shortening
2 tablespoons honey
2 tablespoons unsulphured molasses
1 egg, unbeaten
1½ cups sifted all-purpose unbleached flour
2 teaspoons double-acting baking powder
½ teaspoon baking soda
½ teaspoon salt
¾ cup buckwheat groats (kasha)
1 cup buttermilk
¼ cup cut seeded raisins

Cream shortening, honey, and molasses until light and fluffy. Beat in egg. Sift flour, baking powder, soda, and salt. Blend into shortening mixture. Add buckwheat groats, buttermilk, and raisins; mix only until dry ingredients are moistened. Half-fill oiled 2½-inch muffin pans with batter. Bake in hot oven (425°F.) 20 minutes, or until baked and browned. Yield: 12 muffins.

GOLDEN OATMEAL MUFFINS

1 cup sifted all-purpose unbleached flour
1 tablespoon baking powder
½ teaspoon salt
1 cup oats, uncooked
3 tablespoons vegetable oil
¼ cup honey
1 egg, beaten
1 cup milk

Sift together flour, baking powder, and salt into a bowl. Stir in oats. Add remaining ingredients; stir only until dry ingredients are moistened. Fill oiled medium-sized muffin cups ⅔ full. Bake in preheated hot oven (425°F.) about 15 minutes. Serve piping hot. Yield: 12 muffins.

FRUIT OR NUT MUFFINS: Add ½ cup raisins, chopped, pitted dates, or nutmegs with the oats.

CINNAMON-TOPPED MUFFINS: Combine 2 tablespoons honey, 2 tablespoons all-purpose unbleached flour, 1 teaspoon cinnamon, and 1 teaspoon melted butter or margarine. Sprinkle over muffins before baking.

OATMEAL YEAST ROLLS

1 cake compressed or 1 package dry yeast
¼ cup lukewarm water
¾ cup milk, scalded
¼ cup honey
2 teaspoons salt
⅓ cup butter or margarine
1 egg
4½ to 5 cups sifted all-purpose unbleached flour
1 cup cooked oatmeal, cooled

Soften yeast in lukewarm water. (Use warm water 110°–

115°F. for dry yeast.) Pour scalded milk over honey, salt, and butter. Cool to lukewarm. Stir in egg and 1 cup flour. Add softened yeast and oatmeal. Stir in enough additional flour to make a soft dough.

Turn out on lightly floured board or canvas; knead until smooth and satiny, about 10 minutes. Round dough into ball; place in oiled bowl; brush lightly with *melted shortening*. Cover and let rise in warm place until doubled in size, about 1 hour.

Punch dough down; cover; let rest 10 minutes. Shape dough to form crescents, spirals, cloverleaf, or Parker House rolls. Place cloverleaf rolls in oiled muffin cups; place other shapes on oiled cooky sheets. Brush with *melted shortening*. Cover; let rise in warm place until nearly doubled in size, about 45 minutes. Bake in preheated moderate oven (375°F.) 15 to 18 minutes or until golden brown. Yield: 3½ dozen rolls.

SCOTCH SCONES

    1½ cups sifted all-purpose unbleached flour
    1 tablespoon baking powder
    ¾ teaspoon salt
    ⅓ cup shortening
    ½ cup oats, uncooked
    ¼ cup currants
    ¼ cup honey
    ⅔ cup milk

Sift together flour, baking powder, and salt into bowl. Cut in shortening until mixture resembles coarse crumbs. Stir in oats and currants. Add honey and milk; stir only until dry ingredients are moistened. Turn out on lightly floured board or canvas. Knead gently a few seconds. Roll out to ¼ inch thickness. Cut with floured diamond-shaped cutter. Brush lightly with melted butter; drizzle with honey. Place on unoiled cooky sheet. Bake in preheated hot oven (425° F.) 12 to 15 minutes. Serve piping hot. Yield: 12 scones.

PECAN LOAVES

1½ cups sifted all-purpose unbleached flour
1 tablespoon baking powder
1 teaspoon salt
½ teaspoon mace
½ teaspoon nutmeg
½ cup honey
1 cup chopped pecans
1½ cups oats, uncooked
1⅓ cups milk
1 egg, beaten
¼ cup vegetable oil

Sift flour, baking powder, salt, and spices together into bowl. Stir in honey, pecans, and oats. Add remaining ingredients; stir only until dry ingredients are moistened. Pour batter into 3 oiled empty cans, about 2 cups capacity. Bake in preheated moderate oven (350°F.) about 50 minutes. Loosen edges; remove from cans immediately; cool thoroughly. Wrap cooled bread and store one day before slicing. Yield: 3 loaves. NOTE: For variety, use 1 cup chopped pitted dates or prunes in place of the pecans in above recipe.

BASIC CORN BREAD

1 cup milk, whole or skim
1 beaten egg
⅓ cup honey
2 tablespoons oil
1 cup undegerminated yellow corn meal
1 cup unsifted all-purpose unbleached flour
4 teaspoons double-acting baking powder

Preheat oven to 400°F. (hot). Oil an 8 x 8 x 2-inch baking pan. Combine milk, egg, and honey; stir in oil. Now add liquid mixture to dry ingredients; stir only enough to mix. Pour batter into pan. Bake 20 to 25 minutes, or until lightly browned. Yield: 6 servings, 4 by 2½ inches each.

VARIATION: To make corn muffins, fill oiled muffin tins half full of batter. Bake at 400°F. (hot oven) 20 to 25 minutes. Yield: 12 muffins.

OATMEAL-RAISIN MUFFINS

1 egg, slightly beaten
1 cup milk
¼ cup honey
⅓ cup oil
1¼ cups unsifted all-purpose unbleached flour
1 cup rolled oats, uncooked
1 tablespoon double-acting baking powder
½ cup seedless raisins

Preheat oven to hot (400°F.). Oil muffin tins. Now combine egg, milk, and honey. Add oil. In another bowl, mix rest of ingredients thoroughly. Add liquid to dry ingredients. Stir until dry ingredients are barely moistened. Do not overmix. Batter should be lumpy. Fill muffin tins half full of batter. Bake 20 to 25 minutes, or until golden brown. Yield: 12 medium-sized muffins.

JOHNNY CAKE

⅔ cup unsifted all-purpose unbleached flour
1½ cups yellow undegerminated corn meal
1½ teaspoons double-acting baking powder
¾ teaspoon baking soda
2 eggs, well-beaten
1¼ cups buttermilk or yoghurt
1 tablespoon honey
¼ cup oil

Preheat oven to hot (400°F.) Oil an 8 x 8 x 2-inch baking pan. Now mix dry ingredients thoroughly. Combine eggs, buttermilk and honey; add to flour mixture and stir until well mixed. Stir in oil. Pour into prepared pan. Bake 30 to 35 minutes. Yield: 1 loaf. NOTE: To sour whole or skim milk, place 4 teaspoons vinegar or lemon juice in a 2-cup measure and add milk to the 1¼ mark. Let stand at least 5 minutes.

CHAPTER 11

MAIN DISHES

BEEF LOAF

1 pound ground beef, regular or lean
½ cup rolled oats or rolled wheat, uncooked
¾ cup cooked tomatoes
¼ cup yoghurt or buttermilk
⅛ teaspoon paprika
2 tablespoons finely chopped onion

Preheat oven to moderate (350°F.). Mix all ingredients thoroughly. Lightly pack mixture into 9 x 5 x 3-inch loaf pan. Bake 1¼ hours, or until done. Let stand 10 minutes; then invert beef loaf on serving platter and slice. Serve with broccoli, potatoes au gratin, lettuce wedges, and fruit. Serves 6.

BRAN-CHICKEN CASSEROLE

FILLING:

1 tablespoon onion, finely chopped
2 or 3 tablespoons chicken fat or oil
¼ cup all-purpose unbleached flour, unsifted
1 cup chicken broth
1 cup milk, skim or whole
1 10-ounce package frozen peas and carrots
1½ cups chicken, cooked, diced

TOPPING:

1 cup bran flakes

½ teaspoon poultry seasoning
1 tablespoon parsley, minced
3 tablespoons pimiento, chopped
2 or 3 tablespoons melted margarine

Preheat oven to moderate (375°F.). Cook onion in chicken fat or oil in 2-quart saucepan until tender. Blend in flour. Stir in broth and milk slowly. Cook over moderate heat until thickened, stirring constantly. Add peas and carrots. Cook over low heat, stirring occasionally, for 5 minutes. Add chicken. Pour into 1½-quart casserole. Now combine topping ingredients; mix. Spread over chicken mixture. Bake until the filling bubbles and the topping is crisp, 20 to 30 minutes. Serves 6.

SPECIAL STUFFED PEPPERS

6 medium-sized green peppers
Boiling water
1½ lbs. ground beef
¼ cup chopped celery
¼ cup chopped onion
¾ cup oats, uncooked
1 teaspoon basil
½ cup tomato juice
1 10-oz. can condensed cream of mushroom soup
⅓ cup milk

Cut ¼-inch slice from top of each green pepper; remove seeds and membranes. Cook green peppers about 5 minutes in enough boiling water to cover them; drain. Now sauté ground beef, onion, and celery until lightly browned. Add remaining ingredients; combine thoroughly. Fill green peppers with meat mixture. Stand upright in shallow pan; add small amount of water. Bake in preheated moderate oven (350°F.) about 30 minutes. Serve hot with mushroom sauce made by heating together mushroom soup and milk. Serves 6.

SAUSAGE-APPLE-STUFFED SQUASH

3 large acorn squash, halved and seeded
1½ lbs. sausage meat
¾ cup oats, uncooked
½ cup chopped apple
¼ cup chopped onion
1 tablespoon finely chopped parsley
½ cup milk

Place squash, cut side down, in shallow baking pan. Pour a little water in pan. Bake in preheated moderate oven (350°F.) about 30 minutes. While squash is baking, make sausage balls. Now combine sausage, oats, apple, onion, parsley, and milk thoroughly. Shape to form 18 balls. Brown lightly in small amount of shortening in large skillet. Remove squash from oven; turn cut side up. Place 3 sausage balls in center of each squash. Continue to bake about 40 minutes longer or until squash is tender. Serves 6.

PEANUT BUTTER LOAF

2 cups grated raw carrots
1 cup cooked brown rice
½ cup shelled peanuts (liquefy in blender or chop fine)
½ cup bran
3 tablespoons chopped onion
1 cup milk
3 tablespoons oil
⅛ teaspoon sage

Mix all together. Cover and let stand for 30 minutes. Pour into oiled baking dish. Cover and bake at 350°F. for 1 hour. Serves 4.

WALNUT ROAST

1½ cups soy milk
1 cup bread crumbs

1 cup bran
1 cup ground walnuts
1 medium onion, chopped fine
2 tablespoons oil
2 tablespoons parsley, chopped fine

Sauté the onions in the oil. Mix all ingredients together. Let stand 30 minutes, covered. Turn into an oiled baking dish. Bake for 1 hour at 350°F. Serves 4. NOTE: Pecans may be used instead of walnuts.

BRAN-CHEESE BEAUTY

1 cup cottage cheese
½ cup bran
1 tablespoon oil
2 tablespoons milk
2 teaspoons chopped chives
½ teaspoon chopped parsley

Combine all ingredients and turn into a skillet. Let simmer on stove top. Turn carefully with a spatula. When crisp, remove. Serve hot. Serves 4.

ALMOND LOAF

1 cup whole-grain bread crumbs
1 cup bran flakes
1 cup ground almonds
¾ cup minced celery
2 teaspoons chopped parsley
¼ cup tomato juice
½ cup minced green onions
2 teaspoons brewer's yeast
1 cup milk

Mix all ingredients together and shape into a loaf. Turn into oiled baking dish. Let stand for 30 minutes, uncovered. Bake at 325°F. for one hour. Serves 4.

NUT STUFFED CABBAGE LEAVES

3 cups cooked brown rice
½ cup ground cashew nuts
½ cup bran
½ cup chopped parsley
½ cup chopped celery
½ cup minced onion
1 tablespoon vegetable oil
⅔ cup tomato wedges
Green cabbage leaves

Mix all ingredients except cabbage together and let stand covered for 30 minutes. Now parboil large green cabbage leaves just until soft and easy to handle without breaking. Oil a pyrex or any flat baking dish, lay in cabbage leaf, and stuff with above mixture. Roll up and secure each leaf with a skewer or toothpick and bake at 375°F. for 45 minutes to one hour. Serves 4 to 6.

LENTIL PATTIES

1 medium-sized onion, chopped
2 tablespoons oil
1 cup walnut meats, mashed
3 stalks of celery, chopped
2 cups finely ground whole-grain bread crumbs
1 cup bran
1 tablespoon dried parsley
1½ cups cooked mashed lentils
1 cup water or more to make right moisture to mold into patties

Sauté chopped onion in oil. Turn into mixing bowl and add walnut meats and celery. Combine. Now add all remaining ingredients. Let stand in covered bowl for 30 minutes. Form into patties. Place in oiled pan. Let bake at 375°F. for 45 minutes. Serves 4.

SUNFLOWER LOAF

1 cup ground walnuts
1 cup bran
½ cup grated raw potato
1 teaspoon salt
1 cup milk
3 tablespoons grated onion
½ cup ground sunflower seeds
1 tablespoon oil

Mix all ingredients well. Let stand with cover for 30 minutes. Bake at 350°F. for 1 hour. Serves 4.

PECAN CROQUETTES

1 cup chopped pecans
1 cup cooked brown rice
1 cup bran
1 cup milk
1 tablespoon all-purpose unbleached flour
1 tablespoon finely chopped parsley

Combine all ingredients. Shape into croquettes. Place in oiled pan. Brush top with oil using pastry brush. Bake in preheated oven at 350°F. until golden brown, about 45 minutes. Serves 4.

BRAN BURGERS

½ cup walnuts
1 medium small raw potato
4 tablespoons vegetable oil
1 cup cooked oatmeal
1 cup bran
1 teaspoon brewer's yeast
¼ cup hot water
1 teaspoon all-purpose unbleached flour
Milk, enough to moisten

Grind nuts and potato. Add all other ingredients, dissolving the yeast in ¼ cup hot water. Add enough milk to moisten ingredients, then cover and set aside for 30 minutes. Form into patties and broil, braise in very little oil until golden brown. Serves 4.

CARROT-RICE LOAF

1 cup milk
½ cup peanut butter
2 cups grated carrots
1 cup cold cooked brown rice
2 teaspoons grated onion
½ cup bran
3 tablespoons vegetable oil

Mix milk and peanut butter to a smooth paste and add with other ingredients. Bake slowly at 325°F. for 1 hour in oiled baking dish. Serves 4.

PEANUT ROAST

1 cup milk
½ cup peanut butter
3 tablespoons oil
2 cups grated raw carrots
1 cup cooked brown rice
2 tablespoons grated onion
½ cup bran

Cream milk and peanut butter. Add oil, then other ingredients. Turn into oiled baking dish. Bake slowly at 375°F. for one hour. Serves 4.

STUFFED PEPPERS

4 green peppers
Boiling water
2 cups cooked mashed soy (or other) beans
½ cup finely chopped celery
½ cup finely shredded carrots
¼ cup minced onion
½ cup finely chopped walnuts
½ cup bran
¼ cup tomato sauce or tomato pulp

Remove seeds and membranes from inside of green peppers. Parboil peppers for 3 minutes. Drain. Now fill with mixture of mashed beans, celery, carrots, onions, walnuts, and bran, and moisten with tomato sauce. Top with bread crumbs. Bake 30 minutes at 325°F., or until peppers are soft. Serves 4.

BRAN-NUT-CHEESE LOAF

4 tablespoons butter or margarine
4 teaspoons chopped onion
2 cups grated cheese
2 cups coarsely chopped walnut meats
1 cup bran
1 cup cooked brown rice
1½ cups hot milk
4 eggs, well beaten
2 tablespoons lemon juice

Heat butter in skillet and braise onion until slightly brown. Combine cheese, walnuts, bran, rice, and milk and add to onion and butter. Mix lightly. Fold beaten eggs and lemon juice into mixture. Place in well-oiled loaf pan and bake in slow oven (300°F.) for 45 minutes. Serves 4 to 6.

CHAPTER 12

MEAT

BEEF PATTIES WITH BRAN STUFFING

1 tablespoon butter or margarine
1 cup soft whole-grain bread cubes
½ cup rolled oats or rolled wheat, uncooked
½ cup bran
2 tablespoons chopped onion
¼ teaspoon basil
2 tablespoons warm water
1¼ lbs. ground lean beef
1 cup tomato sauce

Melt butter in a saucepan. Add bread cubes. Heat, stirring constantly until bread is toasted. Add rolled oats, bran, onion, basil, water. Mix. Now preheat oven to moderate (375°F.). Shape beef into 12 patties, each about 3½ inches in diameter. Place the stuffing on six of the patties. Put remaining six patties on top and press edges of meat together around stuffing. Place patties in a shallow pan and top with tomato sauce. Bake for 40 to 45 minutes until meat is lightly browned. Add a little water if sauce is too dry. Serves 6.

SAVORY MEAT LOAF

1½ pounds chopped beef
½ cup buckwheat groats (kasha)
2 eggs
1 medium onion, chopped

142

½ green pepper, chopped, seeded
1½ teaspoons salt
½ teaspoon poultry seasoning
1½ cups tomato wedges

Combine ingredients and mix lightly. Pack into oiled 9 x 5 x 3-inch loaf pan. Bake in moderate oven (325°F.) 1½ hours. Serves 4 to 6.

STUFFED VEAL BREAST

1 egg, beaten
½ cup buckwheat groats (kasha)
1 large onion, chopped
1 clove garlic, minced
¼ cup shortening
1 cup water
¼ cup bran
2 eggs, beaten
1 small carrot, shredded
1 2½ pound veal breast
Paprika

Combine 1 egg and groats. In medium sized frying pan, cook onion and garlic in shortening 3 minutes. Stir in groat mixture and water; bring to boil. Cook, tightly covered, over low heat 15 minutes. Add bran, and 2 eggs, carrot and mix well. Cut a deep pocket in veal breast between meat and bone; stuff with groat mixture. Sew pocket with string or close with skewers. Place veal on rack in baking pan; sprinkle with paprika. Roast in moderate oven (325° F.) about 2 hours, or until tender. Serves 4.

SWEET 'N' SOUR MEAT BALLS

1½ pounds chopped beef
½ cup buckwheat groats (kasha)
½ cup bran
2 eggs, beaten
1 medium carrot, grated
1 medium onion, grated
1 clove garlic, minced
¼ cup shortening
1 tablespoon arrowroot powder
1 cup water
⅓ cup vinegar
1 bay leaf, crumbled
1½ tablespoons honey
¼ teaspoon ground cloves
¼ teaspoon ginger

Combine chopped beef, groats, bran, eggs, carrot, onion, garlic and mix well. Shape into 12 meat balls. In large pan, brown meat balls on all sides in shortening. Add arrowroot powder blended with water and remaining ingredients, stirring carefully. Cook, covered, over low heat 30 minutes, or until meat balls are cooked. Serves 4.

GOURMET MEAT LOAF

FILLING:
1 cup fresh or canned sliced mushrooms, drained
½ cup chopped onion
2 tablespoons oil
⅓ cup sour cream

MEAT LOAF:
1½ lbs. ground beef
¾ cup oats, uncooked
1 egg
⅔ cup fruit juice

FOR FILLING: lightly brown mushrooms and onion in oil in a medium-sized skillet. Remove from heat; stir in sour cream.

FOR MEAT LOAF: combine all ingredients thoroughly. Place half of meat mixture in shallow baking pan. Shape to form an oval base. Lengthwise down the center make a shallow "well" for the filling. Shape remaining meat mixture over filling, making sure all filling is covered. Seal bottom and top meat mixtures together. Bake in preheated moderate oven (350°F.) about 1 hour. Let stand 5 minutes before slicing. Serves 6.

MEAT 'N' CHEDDAR LOAF

1½ lbs. ground lean beef
¾ cup oats, uncooked
½ cup grated sharp Cheddar cheese
¼ cup chopped onion
1 egg, beaten
¾ cup milk

Combine all ingredients thoroughly. Pack firmly into an 8½ x 4½ x 2½-inch loaf pan. Bake in preheated moderate oven (350°F.) about 1 hour and 15 minutes. Let stand 5 minutes before slicing. Serves 6.

SURPRISE CHEESEBURGERS

HAMBURGERS:

1½ lbs. ground beef
¾ cup oats, uncooked
1 teaspoon onion powder
2 tablespoons tomato juice
½ cup milk

CHEESY FILLING:

½ cup cottage cheese
2 tablespoons sweet pickle relish

FOR HAMBURGERS: combine all ingredients thoroughly. Shape to form 12 thin patties.

FOR FILLING: combine all ingredients thoroughly. Spread filling on center of 6 of the patties. Cover with remaining patties; pinch edges together to seal. Place in broiler about 4 inches from source of heat. Cook about 7 minutes. Turn and cook about 5 minutes longer. Serve on toasted hamburger buns. Serves 6.

PARTY MEAT BALL APPETIZERS

MEAT BALLS:
    1½ lbs. ground lean beef
    ½ cup oats, uncooked
    1 tablespoon chopped parsley
    ½ cup grated Parmesan cheese
    2 eggs, beaten
    Shortening

SAUCE:
    1 clove garlic, minced
    1 cup tomato wedges
    ½ cup tomato juice
    ½ teaspoon oregano
    ¼ teaspoon basil

FOR MEAT BALLS: combine all ingredients thoroughly. Shape to form small meat balls, using about 1 tablespoon of mixture for each. Brown in small amount of shortening in large skillet, turning frequently until browned on all sides.

FOR SAUCE: combine all ingredients. Pour over browned meat balls; simmer about 30 minutes. Serve in chafing dish. Makes 4 dozen small meat balls.

MEAT BALL STROGANOFF

MEAT BALLS:
    1½ lbs. ground lean beef
    ¾ cup oats, uncooked
    ½ cup milk

SAUCE:
    1 10½-oz. can condensed cream of mushroom soup
    1 cup water
    1 4-oz. can mushroom stems and pieces with liquid
    2 tablespoons tomato paste
    1 tablespoon all-purpose unbleached flour
    2 tablespoons cold water
    ¼ cup sour cream

FOR MEAT BALLS: Combine all ingredients thoroughly. Shape to form 24 meat balls. Brown in small amount of shortening in large skillet.

FOR SAUCE: Combine soup, water, and mushrooms with liquid and tomato paste. Pour over browned meat balls. Cover and simmer about 30 minutes. Combine flour with 2 tablespoons cold water; add to sauce; blend well. Simmer about 5 minutes or until thickened. Just before serving, stir in sour cream. SUGGESTION: Serve over steaming brown rice. Serves 6.

SPICY MEAT BALLS 'N' SAUCE

MEAT BALLS:
    1½ lbs. ground lean beef
    ¾ cup oats, uncooked
    ¼ cup chopped onion
    ¼ teaspoon oregano
    1 egg
    ½ cup milk
    Shortening

SAUCE:

    ½ cup chopped onion
    ⅓ cup chopped green pepper
    1 1-lb. can tomatoes
    1 cup tomato purée
    ¼ teaspoon garlic powder
    ¼ teaspoon cayenne
    ¼ teaspoon oregano
    1 bay leaf

FOR MEAT BALLS: Combine all ingredients thoroughly. Shape to form 12 meat balls. Brown in small amount of shortening in large skillet. Remove meat balls.

FOR SAUCE: Lightly brown onion and green pepper in meat ball drippings. Add remaining ingredients; simmer over low heat about 15 minutes. Add meat balls to sauce; cover and simmer about 45 minutes. Remove bay leaf. SUGGESTION: Serve over steaming brown rice. Serves 6.

SAUCY BEEF BAKE

    ¾ cup bran
    1 cup unbleached elbow macaroni, uncooked
    2 cups tomato purée
    2 eggs
    ⅓ cup finely chopped onion
    ¼ teaspoon sage
    1 teaspoon chili powder
    2 tablespoons Worcestershire sauce
    2 teaspoons parsley flakes
    1½ pounds ground lean beef

Have bran ready and waiting. Now cook macaroni just until tender. Drain well and set aside. In mixing bowl, combine 1 can of tomato purée, eggs, onion, and seasonings. Now add bran; beat well. Add ground beef and cooked macaroni; mix thoroughly. Press firmly and evenly into round oiled 2-quart baking dish or 8-inch ring mold. Bake in moderate oven (350°F.) about 1 hour. Meanwhile, heat remaining 1 cup tomato purée to serve as accompaniment. After removing from oven, let stand about 5 minutes. Invert onto heated platter and unmold. Garnish with parsley. Serves 8.

FAVORITE MEAT LOAF

1 cup bran
1½ lbs. ground lean beef
1 egg, slightly beaten
½ cup finely chopped onion
½ cup finely cut celery
½ cup cooked tomatoes
½ cup milk

In mixing bowl combine all ingredients in order listed, mixing well. Pack lightly in unoiled 9 x 5 x 3-inch loaf pan. Bake in moderate oven (375°F.) about 1 hour. After removing from oven, let stand in pan about 5 minutes before turning out onto heated platter. Slice and serve. Serves 8.

HERBED MEAT SQUARES

1 cup cooked tomatoes
1 cup bran
⅛ teaspoon thyme
⅛ teaspoon oregano
⅛ teaspoon rosemary
2 tablespoons finely chopped onion
1 egg
1½ lbs. ground lean beef
½ cup canned mushroom sauce

Heat tomatoes in 3-quart saucepan. Add bran, seasonings and onion; beat until well-blended. Add egg and beat well. Add meat; mix until thoroughly combined. Pack lightly into 9 x 9-inch baking pan. With handle of wooden spoon, cut into 9 squares and around outside edges. Spoon sauce evenly over meat. Bake in moderate oven (375°F.) about 45 minutes or until done. Serves 9.

ORIENTAL MEATBALLS

> 1 cup bran
> 2 cups tomato purée with mushrooms
> 1 lb. ground lean beef
> 1 egg
> 1 tablespoon soy sauce
> 1 5-oz. can (⅔ cup) water chestnuts, drained and chopped
> ½ cup water

Combine bran and 1 cup of tomato sauce in medium-sized bowl. Let stand until soft; beat well. Add beef, egg, soy sauce, and water chestnuts; mix thoroughly. Shape level measuring tablespoons of meat mixture into small balls; place in shallow baking pan. Combine remaining tomato sauce with water; pour over meatballs. Bake in moderate oven (350°F.) about 40 minutes. Serve with brown rice or unbleached noodles. Serves 6.

VEAL SCALOPPINI

> 1 cup bran
> 2 lbs. boneless veal cutlets, ¼-inch thick
> 1 clove garlic, quartered
> ½ cup olive oil
> 2 cups fresh mushrooms, sliced
> 1 10½-oz. can (1¼ cups) beef bouillon
> 1 tablespoon lemon juice

Set aside bran. Now cut veal into pieces of similar size and shape. Sprinkle bran over veal; pound with meat mallet. Repeat on other side of meat. Cook garlic in heated olive oil in skillet until browned. Add veal and sauté until golden brown on both sides and thoroughly cooked, about 4 minutes. Remove veal to hot platter. In same skillet, cook mushrooms until browned. Add bouillon and lemon juice to mushrooms; heat until bubbly. Pour sauce over veal. Serves 6.

BRANBURGERS

    1 lb. ground lean beef
    ½ cup bran
    ¼ cup vegetable juice
    2 tablespoons tomato juice
    1 tablespoon grated onion
    6 hamburger buns, split

Combine all ingredients, mixing well. Shape into patties. Broil or grill until done as desired. Place between buns. Serves 6.

WHEAT-BRAN-MEAT LOAF

    1 lb. ground lean beef
    ½ lb. ground lean veal
    ½ cup wheat germ
    ½ cup bran
    ¾ cup tomato juice
    1 egg
    1 tablespoon Worcestershire sauce
    1 tablespoon chopped onion

Combine all ingredients in large bowl, mixing well. Shape firmly into a round, flat loaf about 1-inch thick. Place in heavy 10-inch skillet or electric frypan. Cut almost through meat loaf with knife into desired number of pie-shaped servings. Cover and simmer for 30 minutes or until meat is done as desired. Serves 6 to 8.

CHAPTER 13

POULTRY

BRAN-CRISPED CHICKEN

3 lbs. frying chicken pieces
½ cup tomato juice
1 cup bran
Melted margarine or oil

Wash and dry chicken pieces. Dip pieces in tomato juice, then roll in bran. Place chicken pieces skin up in single layer in foil-lined pan; do not crowd. Drizzle with melted margarine or oil. Bake in moderate oven (350°F.) about 1 hour or until tender. No need to turn chicken while cooking. Serves 6.

CHICKEN HAWAIIAN

3 pounds frying chicken pieces
1 egg
½ cup frozen pineapple-orange juice concentrate, thawed
1 cup bran
½ cup shredded coconut
½ teaspoon curry powder
¼ cup margarine, melted
Lettuce leaves

Arrange chicken pieces in shallow baking pan. Now beat egg with pineapple-orange juice in small bowl and pour over chicken pieces; let stand in refrigerator about 1 hour, turning pieces once. In shallow dish or pie pan, mix bran with coconut and curry. Drain chicken pieces slightly; coat with bran mixture. Place skin side up in single layer in foil-lined shallow baking pan. Drizzle with melted margarine. Bake in moderate oven (350°F.) about 1 hour or until fork tender. Serve on heated plates. Garnish with pineapple ring twists dipped in coconut and placed on lettuce leaves. Serves 6 to 8.

SAVORY CHICKEN DIVAN

½ cup regular margarine or butter
½ cup all-purpose unbleached flour
2 cups water
2 chicken bouillon cubes
1 cup bran
1 10-oz. package frozen broccoli spears, cooked and drained*
8 large slices cooked chicken or turkey breasts
¼ cup grated Parmesan cheese

Melt margarine in saucepan; stir in flour. Add water gradually, stirring constantly; add bouillon cubes. Cook until thickened, stirring occasionally. Spread bran on bottom of oiled 1½-quart baking dish. Pour half of sauce over the bran. Arrange broccoli over bran and sauce, top with a layer of chicken slices, cover with remaining sauce. Sprinkle with cheese. Bake in moderate oven (350°F.) about 20 minutes or until thoroughly heated. Serves 4 to 6.

---

* *Fresh broccoli may be used in place of frozen.*

GRILLED CHICKEN WITH BRAN

1 egg, beaten
1 cup bran
1 medium onion, chopped
¼ cup shortening
3 chicken bouillon cubes
3 cups hot water
⅛ teaspoon rosemary
1½ cups finely chopped cooked chicken
Whole wheat flour
Oil for frying

Combine egg and bran. In medium-sized frying pan, cook onion in shortening 3 minutes. Stir in bran mixture, chicken bouillon cubes dissolved in water, and rosemary; bring to boil. Cook, tightly covered, over low heat 15 minutes. Add chicken; mix well. Spread evenly in oiled 9 x 5 x 3-inch loaf pan. Chill. Unmold. Cut into 8 to 12 slices. Dredge in flour; brown on both sides in hot oil. Serves 4.

BRAN CROQUETTES

2 cups cooked bran
2 cups ground cooked chicken
2 tablespoons chopped onion
Whole-grain bread crumbs
1 egg, beaten

Combine bran, chicken, onion. Chill; shape to form 12 croquettes. Roll in bread crumbs. Dip in egg and roll again in bread crumbs. Pan broil in hot shortening until golden brown, turning only once. Serves 6.

COUNTRY FRIED CHICKEN

3 lbs. broiler-fryer chicken, cut up
½ cup bran

½ cup all-purpose unbleached flour
1 teaspoon paprika
Cooking oil or melted shortening

Wash chicken pieces and pat dry with paper towel. Measure dry ingredients into paper or plastic bag. Shake well to blend. Place chicken pieces in bag, a few at a time. Shake until coated with bran mixture. Preheat oil (½ inch deep) in skillet to 375°F. Sauté coated chicken pieces for 30 to 35 minutes or until done as desired. Turn several times to brown on all sides. Serves 6 to 8.

LEMON-FLAVORED CHICKEN

¼ cup lemon juice
¼ cup vegetable oil
¼ teaspoon thyme
1 2½ - to 3½ -pound frying chicken, cut in quarters
½ cup bran
¼ cup oil

Combine lemon juice, oil, and thyme to make marinade. Pour over chicken. Be sure all chicken parts are in contact with marinade. Let marinate for 1 hour in refrigerator. Drain chicken. Cover with bran. Heat oil in heavy skillet. Place chicken in hot oil and sauté until golden brown on all sides. Bake in moderate (350°F.) oven about 30 minutes or until tender. Serves 4.

BRAISED CHICKEN—CHINESE STYLE

1 2½ - to 3½ -lb. frying chicken, cut up
1 clove garlic, crushed
3 tablespoons vegetable oil
½ pound mushroom caps
½ cup bran
2 tablespoons soy sauce

Brown chicken and garlic lightly in oil. Add mushrooms. Dust with bran and cover. Cook 5 minutes. Add soy sauce. Now cover and cook gently 20 to 30 minutes or until chicken is tender. Serves 4.

CHICKEN CACCIATORE ·

1 2½- to 3½-lb. frying chicken, cut up
½ cup vegetable oil
½ cup chopped green onion
½ cup chopped celery
2 cloves garlic, chopped
1 4-ounce can button mushrooms
1½ cups tomato wedges
½ cup tomato purée
½ cup bran
2½ cups water
¾ lb. unbleached spaghetti

Brown chicken pieces in oil over medium heat. Remove chicken; add onion, celery, and garlic, and sauté slowly 15 minutes. Stir in mushrooms, tomatoes, tomato wedges, tomato purée. Add water and chicken that has been coated with bran; cook over low heat until chicken is tender. Cook spaghetti, then remove chicken from sauce and place in serving dish. Pour remaining sauce over drained spaghetti. Serves 4.

BRAN-FLAVORED CHICKEN

2- to 3-lb. broiler-fryer chicken
½ cup bran
6 tablespoons oil
4 small white onions, chopped
Chopped parsley
½ cup mushrooms
¼ cup tart apple cider

Cut chicken into quarters. Heat oil. Quickly brown the chicken on both sides. Coat with bran. Now cover, turn the flame low, and cook about 10 minutes. After 15 minutes of total time, add chopped onions, parsley, mushrooms, and tart cider. Cook about 15 minutes more. Serve over brown rice. Serves 4 to 6.

BASIC BRAN CHICKEN

1 broiler-fryer chicken, cut in serving pieces
½ cup bran, seasoned with
1 teaspoon paprika

Roll chicken pieces in seasoned bran. Heat salad oil ½ inch deep in skillet. Place chicken, skin side down, in skillet. Put larger, meatier pieces first. Cook uncovered 15 to 25 minutes on each side, turning only once. Drain well on absorbent paper. Serves 4.

CHICKEN CREOLE

1 broiler-fryer chicken, cut in serving pieces
¼ cup bran
½ teaspoon paprika
2 tablespoons salad oil
¼ cup water
1 medium onion, sliced
1 medium green pepper, seeded and cut in strips
½ cup diced celery
1 pound tomatoes
1 teaspoon dried tarragon
2 tablespoons chopped parsley

Sprinkle chicken pieces with bran and some of the paprika. Place chicken pieces, skin side down, in heated oil in skillet. Brown on both sides; remove from skillet. Add water, scraping brown particles from bottom of pan. Add onion, green pepper, and celery; cover and cook 5 minutes. Add remaining paprika, chicken pieces, tomatoes, and tarragon. Bring to a boil. Cover; reduce heat and simmer 40 minutes. Turn into serving dish; sprinkle with parsley. Serves 4 to 6.

CHICKEN KIEV

½ cup butter or margarine
1 tablespoon chopped chives
1 tablespoon lemon juice
4 whole broiler-fryer chicken breasts, boned
3 eggs, beaten
¼ cup water
2 cups bran

Blend together butter, chives, and lemon juice; chill. Halve breasts, remove skin. Cut through thickest part of each half-breast to form a pocket. Place 1 tablespoon hardened chive butter in each pocket. Combine eggs and water. Dip stuffed chicken breasts in egg mixture, then roll in bran; repeat. Chill 1 hour. Bake in hot oven (350°F.) for 45 minutes or until done. Serves 8.

CHICKEN TANDOOR

2 broiler-fryer chickens, halved
2 large onions, coarsely chopped
2 green peppers, diced
2 tomatoes, sliced
1 tablespoon each: curry powder, coriander, ground cumin
1 teaspoon tumeric
½ teaspoon cinnamon
½ teaspoon garlic
¼ cup vegetable oil
2 cups water
½ cup bran

Place chicken in shallow baking pan. Sprinkle with onion, green pepper, tomato, and spices. Pour in oil. Turn chicken to mix with all ingredients. Cover. Marinate in refrigerator several hours or overnight. Stir in water. Now coat with bran. Bake in moderate oven (375°F.) 50 minutes. If desired, garnish with tomato slices, green pepper rings, and celery stalks. Serves 4.

CHICKEN PAPRIKA

1 broiler-fryer chicken, cut in serving pieces
2 teaspoons paprika
1 cup bran
¾ cup water
¼ cup finely chopped onion
½ cup yoghurt
1 tablespoon chopped parsley

Sprinkle chicken with 1 teaspoon of the paprika. Now coat with bran. Place under broiler heat 10 minutes or until browned, turning once. Put chicken pieces in skillet; add water and onion. Cover; simmer 40 minutes. Remove chicken to serving platter. Add remaining 1 teaspoon paprika, and yoghurt to mixture in skillet. Heat just to serving temperature, stirring constantly; do not boil. Spoon sauce over chicken. Sprinkle with parsley. Serves 4.

THREE-HERB CHICKEN

3 whole broiler-fryer chicken breasts
½ cup bran
¼ teaspoon each: basil, tarragon, and thyme
Juice of ½ lemon or lime
1 tablespoon oil, divided

Halve chicken breasts. Place skin side down on foil-lined broiler pan. Sprinkle with bran and half the herbs. Brush with part of the lemon juice; dot with half the oil. Broil

3 to 4 inches from heat at moderate (350°F.) 30 minutes on each side. Use remaining ingredients after turning. Serves 6.

LUSCIOUS BRAN-CHICKEN

2 eggs, lightly beaten
2½ teaspoons celery powder
1 teaspoon paprika
1 broiler-fryer chicken, cut in parts
2 cups bran
1 cup corn oil

Mix together eggs, celery powder, paprika. Dip chicken in this mixture, then roll in bran. Heat corn oil in deep skillet over medium heat (350°F.). Add chicken. Cook, turning frequently, uncovered, about 45 minutes or until fork can be inserted with ease. Serves 4.

CHICKEN FLAMBÉ

2 broiler-fryer chickens, quartered
¼ cup vegetable oil
⅔ cup fruit juice
4 tablespoons bran
1 cup water
6 tablespoons brandy

Heat oil over medium heat in skillet from which chicken can be served. Add chicken and brown on both sides. Add fruit juice; cover and simmer 45 minutes, or until fork can be inserted with ease. Remove chicken pieces. Stir bran into drippings in pan. Add water and bring to boil. Return chicken to pan. Add brandy, ignite, and serve blazing. Spoon sauce over chicken when serving. Serves 8.

SESAME-BRAN CHICKEN

4 whole broiler-fryer chicken breasts, halved, boned
1 egg, slightly beaten
½ cup whole-wheat flour
1 teaspoon almond extract
¼ teaspoon baking powder
½ cup sesame seed
½ cup bran
1 cup corn oil

Mix together egg, 1 tablespoon flour, almond extract, baking powder to make a batter. Dip chicken pieces in batter; place on waxed paper. Sprinkle both sides with sesame seed and bran. Coat with remaining flour. Heat corn oil in skillet, over medium heat, until it reaches 375°F. Carefully place the coated chicken pieces, a few at a time, into the hot corn oil. Cook 5 minutes, or until golden brown and chicken is done; drain on paper towels. Garnish with parsley. Serves 8. NOTE: Chicken pieces may be prepared and coated, then refrigerated overnight until just before serving time.

SWEET BRAN CHICKEN

1 broiler-fryer chicken, cut in parts
4 tablespoons bran
¼ cup corn oil
½ cup honey
2 tablespoons soy sauce

Place chicken, skin side up, in large shallow baking pan in single layer. Sprinkle with bran; let stand 10 minutes. Stir together corn oil, honey, and soy sauce; drizzle on chicken. Bake, uncovered in 350°F. oven, about 1 hour, or until fork can be inserted with ease; baste frequently. Serves 4.

MANDARIN CHICKEN

1 broiler-fryer chicken, cut in parts
1 cup bran
1½ cups buttermilk
1 cup fruit purée
¼ cup corn oil
2 teaspoons arrowroot powder

Dip chicken in buttermilk and then into bran. Place chicken skin side up in single layer in large shallow baking pan. In a saucepan mix fruit purée, corn oil, and arrowroot. Bring to boil, stirring frequently. Spoon over chicken. Bake in 350°F. oven about 1¼ hours or until fork can be inserted with ease. Serves 4.

GLAZED CHICKEN

8 broiler-fryer chicken thighs
¼ cup corn oil
½ teaspoon onion powder
½ cup orange marmalade
¼ cup sesame seed
¼ cup bran

Brush chicken with corn oil on all sides. Place on rack in broiler pan on lowest rack in broiler. Broil about 20 minutes, basting with corn oil once or twice. Turn and broil about 20 minutes on second side. Spread marmalade on chicken; sprinkle with sesame seed and bran. Broil about 5 minutes watching carefully. Turn; spread with marmalade, sprinkle with remaining sesame seed and bran. Broil about 5 minutes longer or until fork can be inserted with ease. Serves 4.

CHICKEN EXOTIQUE

½ cup all-purpose unbleached flour
½ cup bran
½ teaspoon poultry seasoning
½ teaspoon paprika
1 broiler-fryer chicken, cut in parts
¾ cup corn oil
½ cup tomato juice
¼ cup orange juice
1 tablespoon honey

In a paper bag, mix together flour, bran, poultry seasoning and paprika. Add chicken; shake to coat. Heat corn oil in skillet over medium heat. Add chicken and brown on all sides. In a small saucepan stir together tomato juice, orange juice, and honey. Simmer, stirring occasionally, about 5 minutes. Place chicken in single layer skin side up in large shallow baking pan. Spoon sauce over chicken. Bake in 350°F. oven, uncovered, about 20 minutes. Spoon on remaining sauce; bake about 20 minutes longer or until fork can be inserted with ease. Serves 4.

CHAPTER 14

FISH

TUNA NOODLE CASSEROLE

4 ounces uncooked whole-wheat noodles
¼ cup chopped onion
⅓ cup diced celery
1 tablespoon oil
3 8-oz. cans tomato sauce, Spanish-style
2 cans (6 or 7 ozs. each) tuna, canned, undrained, flaked
½ cup bran
1 tablespoon butter or margarine

Preheat oven to moderate (350°F.). Oil a 2-quart casserole. Cook noodles in boiling water; drain. Cook onion and celery in oil in 1 quart saucepan until tender. Add tomato sauce; heat to boiling. Place alternate layers of noodles, tuna, and hot tomato mixture in casserole. Top with bran. Dot with butter. Bake 20 minutes or until mixture is heated through and crumbs are browned. Serves 6.

CREOLE SHRIMP IN GRITS RING

GRITS RING:
1¼ cups unbolted hominy grits
5 cups boiling water

CREOLE SHRIMP:
½ cup chopped onion
½ cup chopped green pepper

½ cup chopped celery
2 tablespoons butter or margarine
¼ cup all-purpose unbleached flour
2 cups tomato juice
1 clove garlic, minced
2 cups cooked, cleaned shrimp

FOR RING: slowly stir grits into boiling water; cover and cook slowly 25 to 30 minutes, stirring frequently. Pour into oiled 5-cup ring mold; let stand at room temperature about 25 minutes. Unmold onto plate; fill center with creole shrimp.

FOR CREOLE SHRIMP: cook onion, green pepper, and celery in butter until tender. Stir in flour. Gradually add tomato juice, stirring constantly until thickened. Add garlic; mix well. Add shrimp; simmer about 10 minutes. Serves 6.

BRAN-COATED FISH

⅔ cup whole bran
2 lbs. fish fillets
½ cup milk

Put bran in flat bowl. Now dip fish in the milk, then roll in bran. Pan-sauté in hot oil until golden brown on each side. Drain on absorbent paper. Serves 6.

SALMON TIMBALES

1 cup milk
1 cup water
½ cup unbolted hominy grits
1 1-lb. can salmon, drained, boned, and flaked
2 tablespoons chopped onion
2 tablespoons chopped green pepper
2 eggs, beaten

Bring milk, water to boil. Slowly stir in grits. Cover and cook 25 to 30 minutes, stirring frequently. Remove from heat. Stir in remaining ingredients. Spoon into oiled 5-oz. custard cups. Place in holder or directly on oven rack. Bake in preheated slow oven (325°F.) about 30 minutes. Remove from oven; let stand 5 minutes. Unmold. Garnish with bran, if desired. Serves 6.

FISH ROLL-UPS

¼ cup finely cut celery
¼ cup finely chopped onion
2 tablespoons margarine or butter
1 cup bran
½ cup milk
6 fish fillets (1½ lbs.) fresh or frozen
¼ cup margarine or butter, melted

Preheat oven to 375°F. Cook celery and onion in margarine until tender but not browned; remove from heat. Add bran, tossing gently. Lightly mix in milk. Cut fillets to size to fit around sides of 6 well-oiled 2½- to 3-inch muffin-pan or custard cups, overlapping ends of fillets. Fill centers of cups with stuffing; brush with melted margarine. Bake in moderate oven (375°F.) about 25 minutes or until fish flakes easily when tested with a fork. To serve, lift from cups; fish will retain shape. Serves 6.

GOLDEN SALMON STEAKS

1 egg
1 tablespoon water
4 salmon steaks
1 cup bran
Vegetable oil
Lemon wedges

In small bowl, combine egg, water; beat until well-blended.

Dry salmon steaks; dip in egg mixture. Coat generously with bran. Fill heavy skillet with ½ inch of oil. Heat oil to 375°F. Sauté steaks in hot oil about 7 minutes on each side, turning only once; drain. Serve with lemon wedges. Serves 4.

OVEN-CRUSTY FISH

1 pound fish fillets, fresh or frozen
½ cup milk
1 cup bran
4 teaspoons vegetable oil or melted regular margarine

Cut fish into serving pieces allowing about ¼ pound for each serving. Dip fish in milk, then in bran. Arrange on well-oiled baking sheet or shallow pan. Sprinkle fish with vegetable oil. Bake in moderate oven (375°F.) about 20 minutes or until tender. Serves 4.

BAKED SEAFOOD SALAD

1 cup bran
2 tablespoons margarine or butter, melted
1 cup cooked, cleaned shrimp
½ cup chopped green pepper
¼ cup finely chopped onion
1 cup finely cut celery
1 cup mayonnaise
Paprika

Combine bran with melted margarine. Reserve for topping. Put shrimp into mixing bowl. Add remaining ingredients except paprika; mix lightly. Spread in individual shells or 9 x 9-inch shallow baking dish. Sprinkle with buttered bran and paprika. Bake in moderate oven (350°F.) about 30 minutes. Serve with lemon. Serves 6.

CURRIED TUNA SQUARES

1 6-oz. can (1 cup) chunk-style tuna
2 cups cooked brown rice
1 tablespoon chopped onion
1 tablespoon lemon juice
½ teaspoon curry powder
2 eggs, slightly beaten
¾ cup milk
1 cup bran
1 tablespoon regular margarine or butter, melted

Drain and flake tuna; place in mixing bowl. Add rice, onion, lemon juice, curry, eggs, milk, and ¾ of the bran. Mix well. Spread tuna mixture in oiled 10 x 6-inch baking dish. Mix remaining bran with melted margarine; sprinkle over tuna mixture. Bake in moderate oven (350°F.) about 20 minutes. Cut into squares and serve with lemon wedges. Serves 6.

QUICK 'N' EASY SALMON PATTIES

1 1-lb can (2 cups) salmon (or other cooked fish),
    boned, reserve liquid
1 cup bran
2 eggs, slightly beaten
2 tablespoons finely snipped parsley
3 tablespoon finely chopped onion
Vegetable oil

In mixing bowl, combine salmon, ½ cup of the bran, ¼ cup salmon liquid, eggs, parsley, and onion; mix thoroughly. Shape into 12 flat patties, 2½ inches in diameter. Coat with remaining bran. In large skillet, place a small amount of oil. Sauté patties in hot oil on medium temperature approximately 2 minutes on each side or until golden brown. Serve piping hot. Serves 6.

SALMON LOAF WITH EGG SAUCE

1 1-lb. can (2 cups) salmon
2 eggs, slightly beaten
½ cup milk
1 teaspoon finely chopped onion
1 tablespoon finely chopped green pepper
1 teaspoon lemon juice
1 cup bran

Drain salmon; reserve liquid. Remove bones and skin; break salmon into chunks in mixing bowl. Add eggs to salmon and mix well. Stir in remaining ingredients and spread evenly in well-oiled 9 x 5 x 4-inch loaf pan. Bake in moderate oven (350°F.) about 45 minutes. Serve piping hot with Egg Sauce. Serves 6.

EGG SAUCE:

2 tablespoons regular margarine or butter
2 tablespoons all-purpose unbleached flour
¾ cup milk
¼ cup salmon liquid
2 tablespoons lemon juice
1 hard-cooked egg, peeled and chopped
Snipped parsley

Melt margarine in saucepan over low heat; stir in flour and mix well. Add milk and salmon liquid gradually, stirring constantly. Cook until thickened, stirring occasionally. Just before serving, add lemon juice and hard-cooked egg. Garnish with snipped parsley.

TUNA-RICE CASSEROLE

3 tablespoons regular margarine or butter
3 tablespoons all-purpose unbleached flour
2 cups milk
½ teaspoon paprika
2 cups grated Cheddar cheese
2 cups cooked brown rice
1 7-oz. can (1 cup) tuna, flaked
¼ cup snipped parsley
1 cup bran
1 teaspoon regular margarine or butter, melted

To make cheese sauce: melt margarine in saucepan over low heat; stir in flour. Add milk gradually, stirring constantly. Cook until thickened, stirring occasionally. Add paprika and cheese, stirring until cheese is melted.

In oiled casserole, arrange layers of rice, tuna, parsley, and cheese sauce. Combine bran with melted margarine. Sprinkle over tuna mixture. Bake in hot oven (425°F.) about 15 minutes or until thoroughly heated. Serve piping hot. Serves 6.

EASY-TO-DO FISH FEAST

Halibut fillets (or any desired fillets)
Bran
Lemon juice

Sprinkle the fillets with lemon juice and roll in bran. Oil your broiler pan. Broil 4 inches below the flame for 15 minutes, turning once. Serve with lemon juice.

FISH DELIGHT

3 to 4 lbs. of cod, haddock, halibut, or flounder fillets
3 cups milk

¼ cup bran
¼ cup all-purpose unbleached flour
2 tablespoons oil

Steam fish over boiling water until tender. Cool. Flake carefully from the bones; remove skin. Combine milk, bran, and flour, stirring constantly until thick. Oil a baking dish. Lay several spoons of the milk-bran-flour mixture on the bottom; add some of the flaked fish, more sauce, more fish. Top with additional bran, if desired. Bake at 375°F. for 30 to 40 minutes. Serves 4 to 6.

BAKED FISH LOAF

2 cups flaked codfish or salmon
1 beaten egg
⅔ cup milk
1 tablespoon chopped parsley
½ cup unbleached flour
¼ cup bran
¼ teaspoon nutmeg
½ cup cheddar cheese

Combine all ingredients and mix well. Press in loaf pan and bake at 375°F. for about 35 minutes. Serve piping hot. Serves 4 to 6.

CHAPTER 15

SALADS AND MEATLESS MEALS

BULGUR PILAF

1 cup bulgur wheat (couscous), dry, unseasoned
¼ cup onion, chopped
¼ cup green pepper, chopped
2 tablespoons butter or margarine
2 bouillon cubes, beef or chicken flavored
2 cups hot water
1 4-ounce can mushroom stems and pieces, undrained
¼ teaspoon thyme

Preheat oven to moderate (350°F.). Place bulgur wheat in a 1-quart casserole. Now cook onion and green pepper in butter in a skillet until tender, about 6 minutes. Add bouillon cubes and water to skillet. Stir until bouillon cubes are dissolved. Add mushrooms and thyme. Combine mixture with bulgur in casserole. Cover and bake 30 to 40 minutes, or until bulgur is tender. Serves 6.

GREEN BEAN AND MUSHROOM CASSEROLE

1 egg, beaten
1 cup buckwheat groats (kasha)
1 large onion, chopped
½ green pepper, chopped
1 can (2 to 4 oz.) sliced mushrooms, drained
¼ cup shortening
2 cups drained canned or fresh cooked green beans
1 cup water
Shredded cheese

172

Combine egg, buckwheat groats. In medium-sized skillet, cook onion, green pepper, and mushrooms in shortening 3 minutes. Stir in groat mixture, green beans, and water; bring to boil. Cook, tightly covered, over low heat 15 minutes. Turn into serving dish; garnish with cheese. Serves 4 to 6.

BUCKWHEAT AND BOWKNOTS (KASHA VARNISHKAS)

1 egg, beaten
1 cup buckwheat groats (kasha)
1 large onion, chopped
¼ cup shortening
2 cups water
1 cup packaged bowknot noodles or unbleached elbow macaroni

Combine egg, groats. In medium-sized skillet, cook onion in shortening 3 minutes. Stir in groat mixture and water; bring to boil. Cook, tightly covered, over low heat 15 minutes. Cook noodles according to package directions; drain. Add noodles to groats; toss lightly to mix well. Serves 4 to 6.

BAKED STUFFED PEPPERS

4 large green peppers
Boiling water
1 egg, beaten
½ cup buckwheat groats (kasha)
1 large onion, chopped
¼ cup shortening
1 cup water
2 cups cooked brown rice
2 sprigs parsley, chopped
1 8-oz. can tomato sauce
½ cup water

Cut thin slice from stem end of each pepper; remove seeds and membrane. Wash. Parboil peppers in boiling water 5 minutes. Drain. Combine egg and groats. In medium-sized skillet, cook onion in shortening 3 minutes. Stir in groat mixture and 2 cups water; bring to boil. Cook, tightly covered, over low heat 15 minutes. Add rice, parsley; toss lightly to mix well. Stuff peppers with mixture; arrange in shallow baking dish. Blend tomato sauce with ½ cup water; pour around peppers. Bake in moderate oven (350°F.) 30 minutes, or until tender. Serves 4.

BROCCOLI CASSEROLE

1 cup bran
3 tablespoons regular margarine or butter, melted
2 10-oz. packages frozen chopped broccoli, or use fresh
1 cup water
1 cup (4 oz.) cubed American cheese
1 10½-oz. can (1¼ cups) condensed cream of mushroom soup

Toss bran with melted margarine. Set aside. Place broccoli, water in saucepan. Bring to a rolling boil, separating broccoli pieces with a fork. Remove from heat. Drain well; set aside. Place cheese in saucepan; add soup. Cook over medium heat until cheese is melted, stirring frequently. Stir in partially cooked broccoli. Pour into unoiled shallow 1½-quart rectangular baking dish. Sprinkle bran mixture over top. Bake in moderate oven (350°F.) about 20 minutes or until bubbly and hot. Serves 6.

SWISS GREEN BEANS

2 tablespoons regular margarine or butter
2 tablespoons regular all-purpose unbleached flour
½ teaspoon grated onion
1 cup yoghurt
3 cups French-cut green beans, cooked and drained
¾ cup bran
1½ cups grated Swiss cheese

Measure margarine into saucepan; place over low heat until margarine is melted. Stir in flour and onion. Add yoghurt, stir until smooth. Increase heat to medium and cook until sauce is bubbly and thickened, stirring constantly. Fold in green beans. Pour into oiled 1½-quart baking dish. Lightly toss together bran and grated cheese. Sprinkle over beans. Bake in moderate oven (350°F.) about 20 minutes or until bubbly. Serves 6.

FETTUCCINI

½ cup bran
1 cup grated Parmesan cheese
1 12-oz. package unbleached broad egg noodles
½ cup regular margarine or butter, softened
2 tablespoons finely snipped parsley

Mix bran with cheese and set aside. Cook noodles according to package directions until tender. Drain thoroughly, do not rinse. Mix margarine and parsley with hot noodles. Add crumb mixture; toss lightly. Serve piping hot on warm platter. Serves 6 to 8.

COLORFUL POTATO SALAD

⅓ cup French dressing
⅓ cup mayonnaise
3 cups diced cooked potatoes
4 hard-cooked eggs, coarsely chopped
3 cups small-curd cottage cheese, drained
½ cup bran
¼ cup chopped pimiento
⅓ cup chopped green pepper
3 tablespoons minced onion
3 tablespoons chopped parsley
Salad greens
Radishes
Ripe olives

Combine French dressing, mayonnaise in large bowl. Mix well. Stir in potatoes and eggs. Let stand 20 minutes. Add remaining ingredients. Mix well. Press into buttered 1½-quart ring mold. Chill until firm (about 1½ to 2 hours). Unmold by immersing mold up to rim in warm water about 15 seconds. Place serving plate over mold and invert salad onto plate. Garnish with salad greens, radishes, and ripe olives or as desired. Serves 10 to 12.

HAWAIIAN SALAD

1 3-oz. package cream cheese, softened
¼ cup bran
1 tablespoon pineapple syrup
6 sliced pineapple
6 lettuce leaves
Salad dressing, if desired

Combine cream cheese, bran, and pineapple syrup. Mix well. Shape into 1-inch balls. Roll in additional bran, if desired. Arrange pineapple slices on lettuce leaves. Top with cheese balls. Serve with desired salad dressing. Serves 6.

JIFFY JELLIED SALAD

2 3-oz. packages flavored gelatine
¾ cup coarsely chopped fruit or vegetable
½ cup bran
½ cup small-curd cottage cheese
Salad greens
Relishes

Prepare gelatine using the ice cube method as directed on package. Fold in fruit or vegetable, bran, and cottage cheese. Pour into 1½-quart ring mold. Chill until firm, about 1½ to 2 hours. Unmold by immersing mold up to rim in warm water about 10 seconds. Place serving plate over mold and invert salad onto plate. Garnish with salad greens and relishes. Serves 10 to 12.

GINGERED SWEET POTATOES

2 1-lb. 7 oz.-cans sweet potatoes, drained
⅓ cup honey
⅓ cup orange juice
¼ cup melted butter or margarine
1½ to 2 tablespoons finely grated orange rind
2 tablespoons chopped preserved ginger
1 tablespoon preserved ginger syrup (or ½ teaspoon ginger)
1 orange, peeled and sliced

Mash sweet potatoes. Add remaining ingredients, mixing well. Pour into oiled shallow 1½-quart casserole. Cover. Bake at 350°F. for 35 to 40 minutes. Remove from oven. Cut orange slices in half. Arrange slices spoke-fashion over sweet potato mixture. Sprinkle *Bran Topping* between orange slices. Serves 6 to 8.

Bran Topping:
¼ cup melted butter or margarine
¼ cup honey
½ cup bran

Combine butter and honey in saucepan. Cook over medium heat until bubbly. Stir in bran. Use as topping.

VEGETABLE-NUT LOAF

1 cup diced carrots
1 cup diced celery
½ cup chopped onion
⅓ cup butter or margarine
¼ cup all-purpose unbleached flour
1½ cups milk
1 cup grated American cheese
1 cup chopped pecans
¾ cup bran
3 eggs, slightly beaten

Sauté carrots, celery, and onion in butter until onion is tender. Stir in flour. Add milk all at once. Cook over medium heat until mixture thickens, stirring constantly. Add cheese. Stir until melted. Stir in nuts, bran, and eggs. Pour into oiled, foil-lined 9 x 5 x 3-inch loaf pan. Bake at 350°F. for 50 minutes or until firm. Let stand in pan 10 minutes. Turn out onto serving plate. Slice and serve piping hot. Serves 6 to 8.

GOLDEN CHEESE SALAD

1 3-ounce package lemon-flavored gelatin
1 cup boiling water
1½ ounces cream cheese, chilled
⅓ cup nuts (pecans, macadamias, or roasted
    peanuts), chopped
1 8-oz. can diced pineapple, drained
2 cups shredded carrots
Lettuce leaves, as desired

Dissolve gelatin in boiling water. Chill. Cut cream cheese into 18 cubes. Coat cream cheese cubes with nuts and roll into balls. Stir pineapple and carrots into gelatin. Add cream cheese balls. Chill several hours or overnight until firm. Serve on lettuce leaves. Serves 6.

STUFFED DATE SALAD

18 pitted dates
3 tablespoons natural, crunchy peanut butter
2 grapefruit, chilled, sectioned
Salad greens, as desired

Fill the dates with the peanut butter. For each salad, arrange three stuffed dates with grapefruit sections on crisp salad greens. Serves 6.

WALDORF DATE SALAD

Add ½ cup pitted, chopped dates to a tart Waldorf salad. Gently stir in ½ cup pecans, walnuts, or roasted peanuts. Serve immediately. Serves 6.

WALDORF GRAPE SALAD

Add ½ cup seedless, quartered red grapes to Waldorf salad. Gently stir in ½ cup chopped pecans, walnuts or roasted peanuts. Sprinkle with cinnamon, if desired. Serve immediately. Serves 6.

NUT-FILLED PEPPER RINGS

2 3-oz. packages cream cheese
½ cup chopped nut meats
¼ cup bran
2 green peppers

Combine cheese with nut meats and bran. Slice tops from

peppers and scoop out seeds and membranes. Fill peppers with cheese-nut-meat-bran mixture, packing solidly. Slice peppers crosswise. Place on lettuce leaves, making individual servings. Dish of paprika may be added. Serves 2 to 4.

GOLDEN BRAN SALAD

2 cups grated, raw carrots
⅓ cup chopped walnut meats
¼ cup bran
1 chopped green pepper
¼ cup sliced, stuffed olives
1 teaspoon grated onion
¼ cup mayonnaise

Mix all ingredients. Chill. Serve on lettuce. Serves 4.

WALDORF CANTALOUPE SALAD

2 cups diced cantaloupe
1 cup diced fresh peaches
1 cup diced apples
1 cup minced celery
¼ cup French dressing
½ cup chopped nut meats
¼ cup bran

Combine fruits and celery. Marinate in French dressing about 10 minutes. Drain off excess dressing. Add nut meats and bran. Serve on crisp lettuce leaves. Top with French dressing or mayonnaise. Serves 4.

RED AND GREEN SALAD

4 large lettuce leaves
2 large ripe avocadoes

1 medium-sized red onion
¼ cup bran

Lay crisp lettuce on individual salad plates. Cut each avocado in half, peel and seed. Slice red onion into thin rings. Lay several rings of onion on each lettuce leaf. Sprinkle bran over onion rings. Place half avocado on each plate. Serve with favorite dressing. Serves 2 to 4.

CHINESE SALAD

⅓ cup finely chopped Chinese cabbage
1 cup crisp bean sprouts
⅓ cup chopped celery
¼ cup chopped green onions
1 handful very tender China peas
¼ cup bran
10 crisp lettuce leaves

Mix together all ingredients, except lettuce. Lay lettuce leaves on salad plates or platter. Turn salad onto lettuce leaves. Pour any favorite dressing over this. Bean sprouts may be steamed 10 minutes and then chilled for a unique flavor. Serves 4.

CANTON SALAD

1 cup slightly cooked bean sprouts
½ cup diced green pepper
½ cup chopped celery
1 diced cucumber
¼ cup bran
1 cup shredded lettuce
1 cup cooked, chilled peas

Toss all together. Serve with favorite dressing. Serves 2 to 4.

VEGETABLE BOWL SALAD

6 green onions
3 stalks chopped celery
1 shredded carrot
1 thinly sliced onion
6 sliced radishes
1 cup sliced cucumbers
½ cup raw cauliflower
½ cup oil and vinegar dressing
¼ cup bran

Combine all ingredients. Let marinate for 30 to 60 minutes before being served. TIP: For added taste thrill, add lettuce leaves and sliced tomatoes just before serving. Serves 4 to 6.

CHAPTER 16

SOUPS

MUSHROOM SOUP

1 cup chopped mushrooms
1 tablespoon chopped onion
¼ cup margarine
4 cups chicken stock
2 teaspoons fruit juice
1 tablespoon margarine
3 tablespoons whole wheat flour
1 teaspoon bran
1 cup milk

Sauté mushrooms and onions in margarine, until onion is transparent. Add 3½ cups chicken stock and simmer 20 minutes. Add fruit juice. If desired, blend in a blender to make it smooth. To thicken, melt 1 tablespoon margarine and blend in flour and bran until mixture is' smooth. Add ½ cup chicken stock; add this to soup mixture. Stir in 1 cup milk. Serves 4.

GREEK EGG-LEMON SOUP

1 medium-sized lemon
1 egg
2 teaspoons bran
6 cups chicken soup with rice (homemade or canned)

Squeeze lemon and strain the juice. Beat egg and very gradually add lemon juice, beating constantly. Prepare the soup and simmer for 5 minutes. Add bran. With a ladle, gradually add about 2 cups of hot soup to the egg-lemon mixture, stirring constantly. Pour the mixture slowly back into the soup. Heat over a very low heat 2 minutes, stirring continuously. Remove from heat and serve promptly with whole wheat bread slices. Serves 4.

CHICKEN SOUP

1 tablespoon margarine
½ chopped celery and leaves
¼ cup chopped onions
4 frying chicken wings
Water
¾ cup diced potatoes
2 teaspoons bran
1 envelope (.19 ounce) instant chicken-flavored
   broth mix
½ cup cooked peas

Melt margarine in Dutch oven or in large heavy saucepot. Sauté celery and onion, stirring occasionally, about 5 minutes. Add chicken wings and enough water to cover. Simmer mixture for 1 hour 45 minutes, adding water as necessary. Stir in potatoes, bran, and instant chicken-flavored broth mix; simmer 20 minutes longer or until potatoes are tender. Add peas and enough water to make 1 quart of soup. Heat. Serves 4.

GAZPACHO SOUP

1 1-pound can stewed tomatoes
1 10½-oz. can beef broth
1 cup peeled, chopped cucumbers
1 cup chopped celery
1 cup sliced onions
2 tablespoons lemon juice
1 small clove garlic, minced

1 teaspoon bran
Dash paprika

Combine all ingredients in a heavy saucepan. Simmer 10 minutes. Chill. Serves 4.

BOUILLABAISE

1½ lbs. fillet of red fish
½ cup vegetable oil
¼ pound shrimp
¼ pound scallops
1½ tablespoons all-purpose unbleached flour
2 tablespoons bran
½ cup chopped onions
½ cup chopped celery
1½ cloves garlic
1½ cups canned, stewed tomatoes, chopped
2 cups water
½ cup fruit juice
1 bay leaf
1½ tablespoons finely chopped parsley
¼ teaspoon saffron
4 slices whole-grain bread, spread lightly with
   margarine, sprinkled with cheese and toasted
   under the broiler

Sauté all seafood in ¼ cup oil until half done, stir in flour and bran, remove from heat, and put aside. Sauté onion, celery, and garlic in remaining oil. Add tomatoes and cook 5 minutes. Add water and remaining ingredients except cheese toast and simmer a few minutes before adding all seafood. Cook 10 minutes longer and serve with cheese toast on top. Serves 4.

CREAM OF CASHEW SOUP

1 tablespoon butter or margarine
2 tablespoons finely chopped celery
2 tablespoons finely chopped onion
2 tablespoons all-purpose unbleached flour
2 tablespoons bran
1 cup milk
2 cups chicken broth or bouillon
1 cup cashews, finely chopped
Paprika or minced parsley (as desired)

Melt fat in a heavy saucepan. Add celery and onion. Cook, stirring frequently until tender. Blend in flour and bran. Gradually stir in liquids and nuts. Bring to boil, stirring as needed. Cook 1 minute longer. Garnish as desired with parsley or paprika. NOTE: If preferred, grind 1 cup of nuts and use in place of chopped nuts. Reduce flour to 1 tablespoon. Serves 6.

CREAM OF PEANUT BUTTER SOUP

Omit the cashews. Follow above recipe. Reduce flour to 1 tablespoon. Blend in ¾ cup peanut butter before adding liquids.

HEARTY CHICKEN NOODLE SOUP

3 pounds chicken, cut up
Water to cover
1 cup carrots, sliced
1½ cups chopped celery with leaves
½ cup chopped onion
½ teaspoon poultry seasoning
1 teaspoon bran
1 tablespoon dehydrated parsley flakes
2 cup unbleached noodles, uncooked

Simmer the chicken in water in a covered saucepan until tender. (A frying chicken will take about 45 minutes.) Remove chicken from broth and cool enough to handle. Remove skin and bones. Chop the meat. Skim most of the fat from broth. Measure broth. Add water, if needed, to make 5 cups. Bring broth to a boil. Add the chicken, vegetables, poultry seasoning, and bran. Simmer, covered, 20 minutes. Add parsley and noodles. Simmer, uncovered, 10 minutes longer or until noodles are tender. Serves 6.

GROUND BEEF AND RICE SOUP

1 pound ground beef, regular or lean
3 bouillon cubes, beef flavored
6 cups hot water
1 1-lb. can tomatoes, canned, undrained
1 ⅜-ounce envelope dehydrated onion soup mix
1 cup celery, diced
¾ cup brown rice, uncooked
½ teaspoon oregano
1 teaspoon bran

Crumble ground beef into 4-quart saucepan; cook over moderate heat, stirring as needed until meat is lightly browned. Stir in rest of ingredients. Bring mixture to a boil. Reduce heat and simmer 40 to 45 minutes or until rice is tender. Stir occasionally. Serves 10.

CREAM OF CORN SOUP

2 cups milk
2 slices onion, chopped
1 tablespoon shortening
1½ tablespoons all-purpose unbleached flour
2 cups cream-style corn
1 tablespoon bran

Scald milk, with onion in it. Melt shortening in pan, blend

flour with it, then gradually add scalded milk, stirring to prevent lumping. Add corn and bran and pour mixture through colander. Heat to boiling point. Beat with rotary beater just before serving. Serves 4.

LIMA BEAN SOUP

2 or 3 carrots
3 small onions
½ cup uncooked brown rice
1 cup cooked lima beans
1 tablespoon bran
2 tablespoons butter or margarine

Cut carrots and onions into small pieces. Add rice and cook in small amount of water until tender. Mash lima beans and add this to preceding mixture. Add bran and butter. If soup is too thick add a little hot water. (Leftover lima or navy beans may be used in this recipe.) Serves 4.

VEGETABLE BROTH

Tops and leaves 1 bunch celery
1 tomato, diced
1 potato, diced
1 onion, peeled and diced
1 carrot, diced
1 small bunch parsley
6 green beans
1 green pepper, seeded, membranes removed, and diced
1 teaspoon bran
4 quarts water

Combine all ingredients and cook slowly for 2 hours. Strain. This recipe makes about 1 quart clear broth and may be increased proportionately. Serves 4.

EASY BRAN VEGETABLE SOUP

4 stalks celery
4 onions
2 carrots
4 potatoes
2 tablespoons butter or margarine
2 tablespoons bran
½ cup tomato wedges
4 quarts water

Wash and dice celery, onions, carrots, and potatoes. Braise vegetables in butter for 30 minutes, using large heavy kettle or Dutch oven. Add bran, tomatoes, and water and stir well. Simmer slowly over low heat for 90 minutes. Serves 8 to 12.

OATMEAL SOUP

1 large onion
3 stalks celery
3 tablespoons oil
1 cup steel-cut oatmeal
4 cups water
1 bouillon cube or 1 teaspoon soy sauce

Chop onion and celery fine and cook in oil until softened. Add oatmeal and cook, stirring constantly until it browns slightly. Pour in water, add bouillon cube or soy sauce, and bring to a boil. Reduce heat and let simmer for about 30 minutes. Serves 4.

SPLIT PEA SOUP

3 cups split peas
3 quarts of water
2 bay leaves
4 tablespoons oil
4 cloves garlic
3 tablespoons soy sauce
1 medium onion, peeled and chopped fine
1 tablespoon bran
3 cups diced potatoes
1 cup chopped celery (with leaves)
2 cups chopped parsley

Soak peas. Add 3 quarts water and cook together with bay leaves, oil, garlic, soy sauce, and onion. Add bran. Cook until dissolved, then add potatoes, celery, and parsley. Cook slowly until vegetables are tender, about 20 minutes. Serves 4 to 6.

LENTIL SOUP

1 cup lentils
1 large onion
½ cup celery leaves
½ cup parsley
2 teaspoons bran
2 tablespoons oil
½ teaspoon sweet basil

Wash lentils and soak several hours. Chop onion, celery leaves, and parsley very fine. Add bran, vegetables, oil, and basil to lentils. Cook in water in which they were soaked. Simmer until tender. Serves 4.

VEGETABLE-BRAN BROTH

3 cups finely chopped celery
3 cups grated carrots
1 cup spinach
1 cup parsley, chopped fine
¼ cup green onion, chopped fine
1 tablespoon bran
1 cup tomato juice

Simmer all ingredients, except tomato juice, in 2 quarts of water for 15 to 20 minutes. Strain. Add tomato juice. Serves 4 to 6.

TOMATO AVOCADO SOUP

1 quart tomato juice
1 teaspoon bran
1 teaspoon chopped chives
1 ripe avocado
½ cup water
½ cup milk

Heat tomato juice. Add bran and chives. Now liquefy avocado using the water and milk. (If you have no lique-fier, mash and whip avocado with fork.) Pour into heated tomato juice, stirring briskly. Do not let boil. Serves 4 to 6.

NAVY BEAN SOUP

1 cup navy beans
7 cups cold water
⅔ cup diced carrots
⅓ cup diced onions
1 tablespoon oil
2 tablespoons chopped parsley
2 tablespoons bran

Soak beans overnight in cold water. Next morning, bring to a boil and turn flame to simmer. Add all other ingredients and simmer beans gently for several hours. NOTE: The longer and slower these beans are cooked, the better the soup. Add water if needed, but not at the end of the cooking; only in the beginning. Serves 4 to 6.

BOSTON-STYLE POTATO SOUP

    1 cup chopped green onions
    3 cups cubed raw potatoes
    1 teaspoon celery seed
    2 tablespoons vegetable oil
    2 cups water
    1 cup fresh green peas
    1 tablespoon chopped parsley
    1 tablespoon bran
    2 cups milk

Cook onions, potatoes, celery seed, oil, and water together until almost done. Then add peas, and parsley, and bran. When peas are done, turn off heat. Add milk. Stir, then turn heat to low flame. Let simmer but not boil. Serves 4 to 6.

CREAM OF CHESTNUT SOUP

Purée: Shell chestnuts by slitting each one and boiling in water for 5 minutes. Drain off water. Pour cold water over them. They will now shell easily.

Boil the chestnuts in a small quantity of water until soft. Put through sieve.

For each cup of purée, use:

    1 cup water (same water in which chestnuts were
       boiled)
    2 cups milk
    1 tablespoon all-purpose unbleached flour
    1 teaspoon bran
    2 tablespoons margarine

Heat milk in double boiler. Thicken it with the flour and bran. Add remaining ingredients. Serves 4 to 6.

HOMEMADE CHICKEN-RICE SOUP

2 quarts chicken stock
¼ cup carrots, cut small
1 cup chopped celery stalks
1 small onion
1 teaspoon bran
¼ cup raw brown rice

Put cold chicken stock and vegetables into soup kettle. Let simmer until vegetables are about half done. Now add bran and rice and continue cooking until rice is soft. Serves 4 to 6.

SQUASH SOUP

2 cups cooked, mashed squash
3 cups milk
½ cup dry skim milk powder
2 cups water
1 tablespoon whole wheat flour
2 tablespoons bran
2 tablespoons oil
1 teaspoon parsley

Combine all ingredients and heat thoroughly. Garnish with extra parsley sprigs. Serves 4 to 6.

DUTCH BUTTERMILK SOUP

1 quart buttermilk
3 tablespoons honey
1 tablespoon bran
3 eggs
Juice of 1 lemon
Cucumber slices

Put all ingredients into blender and let run until smooth.
Serve chilled with thin cucumber slices. Serves 4.

SWEDISH FRUIT SOUP

¾ cup uncooked brown rice
½ cup currants
½ pound seedless raisins
4 apples
¼ cup honey
3 quarts boiling water
½ pound sun-dried prunes
1 lemon, juice and grated rind
1 tablespoon bran

Soak dried fruits 1 hour in water that has been slightly
simmered. Dice but do not peel apples. Mix all the ingredients and let simmer gently for 45 minutes. Serves 4.

HOMEMADE CORN SOUP

2 cups fresh, frozen or home-canned corn
1 quart milk
2 tablespoon all-purpose unbleached flour
1 tablespoon bran
2 tablespoons oil

Combine corn and milk and let simmer gently for 20 minutes. Slowly blend flour, bran, and oil into corn-milk mixture. Take care it does not become lumpy. Let simmer until done. Serve piping hot. Serves 2.

CREAM OF CHEESE SOUP

2 tablespoons chopped onion
2 tablespoon butter
2 tablespoons all-purpose unbleached flour
2 cups milk
1 teaspoon bran
½ cup cooked carrots, minced
½ cup cooked celery, minced
1 cup shredded Cheddar cheese

Sauté onion lightly in butter. Add flour and milk to make a thin white sauce. Add bran, carrots, celery, and cheese. Blend well and heat until steaming. Serves 4.

CHAPTER 17

DAIRY FOODS

TWO-CHEESE CASSEROLE

1 egg, beaten
1 cup buckwheat groats (kasha)
2 tablespoons bran
1 large onion, chopped
¼ cup shortening
2 cups water
1 8-oz. container dry cottage cheese
1 cup shredded Cheddar cheese
Paprika

Combine egg, groats, bran. In medium-sized skillet, cook onion in shortening 3 minutes. Stir in groats mixture and water; bring to boil. Cook, tightly covered, over low heat 15 minutes. Add cottage cheese; toss lightly to mix well. Turn into 1½-quart baking dish; sprinkle with Cheddar cheese and paprika. Place in broiler under low heat 3 to 5 minutes, or until Cheddar cheese is melted. Serves 4 to 6.

CHEESE LASAGNE

8 ounces lasagne noodles (or any wide noodles)
1 cup tomato purée
1½ cups cottage cheese
½ teaspoon basil
¼ teaspoon Worcestershire sauce
¼ cup finely chopped onion
¼ pound American cheese, thinly sliced
2 tablespoons grated Parmesan or Romano cheese

½ cup buttered bread crumbs
¼ cup bran

Cook noodles in boiling water until tender; drain and rinse. Mix tomato purée with the cottage cheese, basil, Worcestershire sauce, and onion. Arrange alternate layers of noodles, American cheese, and sauce mixture in oiled 2½-quart casserole. Top with crumbs mixed with bran and grated cheese. Bake in moderate (375°F.) oven about 25 minutes. Serves 4.

SWISS FONDUE WITH WINE

1 clove garlic, peeled and cut in half
1 cup dry white wine
1 pound Swiss cheese, shredded
1½ teaspoons arrowroot powder
2 tablespoons Kirsch
⅛ teaspoon nutmeg
1 teaspoon bran
French bread, pulled into pieces

Rub inside of earthenware fondue dish with garlic. Pour in wine. Heat to boiling. Add shredded cheese gradually, stirring constantly, until melted. Blend arrowroot powder with Kirsch and add to cheese mixture. Stirring constantly, bring to boil. Stir until mixture is smooth and thickened. Add seasoning and bran. Lower heat. Serve over heat in warm dish. Use fondue forks to spear bread and dip. Serves 4.

BAKED MACARONI AND CHEESE

1 quart water
3 cups macaroni
1 or 2 cups natural Cheddar cheese, shredded
1 or 2 cups American cheese, shredded
2 eggs, beaten
2 cups milk
1 teaspoon finely chopped onion
¼ cup bran

Bring water to a boil. Add macaroni and cook uncovered, stirring occasionally, until almost tender about 6 minutes. Drain. Now preheat oven to moderate (350°F.). Oil a 1½-quart casserole. Cover bottom of casserole with half the macaroni. Combine cheeses; sprinkle half the mixture over macaroni in casserole. Repeat layers. Combine eggs with milk and onion. Pour over casserole and sprinkle top with bran. Set casserole in pan of hot water. Bake 45 minutes to 1 hour, or until browned and almost set in center. Let cool 10 minutes before serving to allow mixture to set. Serves 6.

HOMINY SOUFFLÉ

2½ cups milk
½ cup unbolted hominy grits
2 tablespoons butter
4 eggs, separated

Scald milk in heavy saucepan. Gradually stir in grits. Cook over low heat 15 minutes, stirring constantly. Remove from heat. Mix in butter until melted. Cool slightly. Beat egg yolks. Gradually stir into hominy. Beat egg whites until stiff but not dry; fold into hominy mixture. Pour into oiled 2-quart casserole and bake in moderate oven (350° F.) 45 minutes or until golden brown. Serves 6.

CHEESE-NOODLE CASSEROLE

3 cups whole-grain noodles
2 tablespoons all-purpose unbleached flour
2 tablespoons bran
1 cup sour cream
1 cup sieved creamed cottage cheese
¼ teaspoon grated onion

Cook noodles in boiling water until just tender. Drain and rinse well. Mix flour and bran in bowl. Add sour cream and stir until smooth. Fold in cottage cheese. Add noodles and onion. Mix well. Turn into buttered shallow 1-quart baking dish. Sprinkle with paprika. Bake in moderate oven (350°F.) 20 minutes or until brown. Serves 6.

WELSH RAREBIT

¼ cup butter
¼ cup all-purpose unbleached flour
2 tablespoons bran
2½ cups milk
1½ cups coarsely grated Cheddar cheese
6 slices whole-grain bread, toasted

Melt butter in heavy saucepan. Stir in flour and bran; mix well. Pour in all of milk and stir vigorously over moderate heat. Continue to cook until thickened, stirring constantly. Add cheese and stir over low heat until cheese is melted. Remove from heat. Mix well. Serve piping hot on toast. Serves 6.

CREAMY CORN TIMBALES

3 eggs
1¼ cups milk, scalded
2 cups cream-style corn
1 tablespoon bran

Beat eggs slightly; gradually add milk, beating vigorously. Add corn, bran. Spoon into buttered individual baking dishes. Bake in pan of hot water in moderate oven (350° F.) about 50 minutes or until set. Garnish with parsley. Serves 6.

COTTAGE PEPPERS

3 peppers, halved, and seeded, with membranes
    removed
2 tablespoons onion, chopped
4 tablespoons butter, melted
2 cups cooked brown rice
1 tablespoon bran
½ teaspoon ground thyme
1¼ cups creamed cottage cheese
⅔ cup tomato purée

Parboil peppers in boiling water 5 minutes. Drain well.
Now cook onion slowly in 2 tablespoons melted butter
until lightly browned, stirring occasionally. Pour over rice.
Add bran, thyme and mix well. Stir in cottage cheese and
tomato purée. Spoon into peppers. Brush filling with remaining butter. Bake in moderately hot oven (375°F.) 30
minutes. Serves 6.

COTTAGE CHEESE CHOPS

4 cups soft whole-grain bread crumbs
1 cup grated cheese
1 cup cottage cheese
5 tablespoons condensed tomato soup
½ cup bran
4 tablespoons shortening
1 egg, slightly beaten

Mix bread crumbs with cheeses, soup, and bran, and shape
into form of chops. Brown on both sides in skillet in hot
shortening. May be served with gravy, if desired. Serves 4
to 6.

CHEESE-NUT LOAF

2 small onions, chopped fine
2 tablespoons butter or margarine
½ cup water
1½ cups bran
1½ cups chopped walnut meats
2 cups grated cheese
Juice of 1 lemon
3 eggs, well beaten
Buttered whole-grain bread crumbs

Sauté onions in butter until light brown. Add water and mix with bran. Add walnuts, cheese, lemon juice, and beaten eggs. Toss together to mix. Turn into oiled casserole, top with buttered crumbs, and bake until brown in hot oven (400°F.). Serves 4 to 6.

CHEESE-BRAN LOAF

1 cup dry cottage cheese
1 cup chopped nut meats
1 teaspoon lemon juice
2 tablespoons tomato juice
1 cup bran
2 tablespoons finely chopped onion
1 tablespoon butter or margarine

Combine all ingredients, mixing thoroughly. Put into well-oiled baking dish and bake in moderately hot oven (375° F.) for 40 minutes or until browned. Serves 4.

CHEESE-BRAN PUDDING

1 cup kernel corn
2 eggs, well beaten
2 tablespoons all-purpose unbleached flour
4 tablespoons bran
2 tablespoons melted butter or margarine
2 tablespoons honey
3 chopped pimientos
Grated cheese

Mix all ingredients except cheese. Pack into oiled baking dish or casserole. Cover with thin layer of grated cheese. Bake in moderate oven (350°F.) about 30 minutes. Serves 2.

FESTIVE BRAN MEAL

2 cups chopped nut meats
1 cup dry whole-grain bread crumbs
1 cup bran
1 tablespoon melted butter or margarine
2 cups milk
1 teaspoon sage
4 eggs, well beaten

Mix all ingredients, adding beaten eggs last. Pour into oiled baking dish. Bake in very hot oven (450°F.) for 15 minutes. Serves 4.

VEGETABLE BAKE

1 3-oz. package cream cheese, at room temperature
1 cup (½ pint) cottage cheese
2 teaspoons lemon juice
½ teaspoons lemon juice
½ teaspoon paprika

¼ teaspoon marjoram
2 eggs, beaten
½ cup soft whole-grain bread crumbs
½ cup bran
1 tablespoon minced onion
2 cups cooked vegetables (peas, corn, green beans,
   carrots, zucchini, etc.)

Preheat oven to 350°F. Blend cream cheese until smooth; mix in remaining ingredients except vegetables. Fold in vegetables and spoon into casserole. Bake 20 to 25 minutes. Serve immediately. Serves 4.

CHEESE-TUNA BAKE

1½ cups creamed cottage cheese
1 7-oz. can tuna, flaked
½ cup bread crumbs
½ cup bran
½ teaspoon celery powder
2 eggs, beaten
2 tablespoons butter

Combine cheese, tuna, ¼ cup crumbs, and celery powder. Blend in beaten eggs. Put in buttered 1 quart casserole. Top with remaining crumbs and bran, mixed with melted butter. Bake at 350°F. about 35 minutes or until firm. Serves 4.

CHAPTER 18

EGGS

EASY EGG CASSEROLE

6 hard-cooked eggs
¼ cup finely chopped celery
1 tablespoon mayonnaise or salad dressing
1 10-oz. can cream of mushroom soup
⅓ cup milk
½ cup grated Cheddar cheese
¼ cup bran
Sliced, stuffed olives

Slice eggs in half, removing yolks. Mash yolks; combine with celery, mayonnaise. Refill whites with yolk mixture. Put two halves together again. Place eggs in a shallow baking dish. Combine the mushroom soup and milk; pour over eggs. Sprinkle with grated cheese and bran. Top with sliced, stuffed olives. Bake in a moderate (350°F.) oven for 30 minutes or until sauce is bubbly. Serves 6.

QUICK EGG SOUFFLÉ

1½ cups milk
2 tablespoons butter or margarine
2 tablespoons bran
6 eggs
Parsley

Heat milk and butter in upper part of double boiler. Add bran to eggs and beat until very light. Add eggs to hot milk and blend well. Cover over gently simmering water for 30 minutes. Serve on warm plates. Garnish with a sprig of parsley or snipped parsley. Serves 6.

EGGS 'N' BRAN CASSEROLE

8 hard-cooked eggs, coarsely chopped
1½ cups diced celery
¼ cup coarsely chopped walnuts
2 tablespoons minced green pepper
1 teaspoon minced onion
⅔ cup mayonnaise or salad dressing
1 cup grated Cheddar cheese
½ cup bran

Combine eggs, celery, walnuts, green pepper, onion and mayonnaise. Toss lightly, but mix thoroughly. Place in oiled 1½-quart baking dish. Sprinkle with cheese and top with bran. Bake in a moderate (375°F.) oven for 25 minutes or until thoroughly heated. Serves 6.

SOUFFLÉ PANCAKES

6 egg yolks
⅓ cup buttermilk pancake mix
¼ cup bran
⅓ cup sour cream
6 egg whites

Beat egg yolks until thick and lemon-colored. Fold in pancake mix, bran, and sour cream until well blended. Beat egg whites until stiff, but not dry. Carefully fold into yolk mixture. Drop by tablespoonful onto hot, well-oiled griddle. Bake until golden brown on both sides. Serve hot with butter, maple syrup, honey, or favorite fruit sauce. Serves 6.

CRISPY TOMATO BAKED EGGS WITH CHEESE

1 cup bran
½ cup grated American cheese
1 tablespoon melted butter or margarine
4 tablespoons tomato juice
1 tablespoon mayonnaise or salad dressing
4 eggs

Toss bran and ¼ cup of the grated cheese with melted butter or margarine. Divide between 4 custard cups (9-oz. size); build up sides to form nests. Place 1 tablespoon of tomato juice in each nest. Divide mayonnaise between the 4 cups. Break one egg into each cup. Top with remaining ¼ cup cheese. Bake in a slow (325°F.) oven for 20 minutes or until eggs cook to desired doneness. Serves 4.

EGGHEAD CUSTARD MOUSSE

2 cups milk
4 egg yolks, beaten
4 tablespoons honey
1 teaspoon vanilla extract
4 egg whites
¼ cup bran

Combine milk, beaten yolks, and honey in saucepan. Cook over low heat until custard coats a spoon and is slightly thickened. Remove from heat immediately; add vanilla and cool. Pour into parfait glasses. Beat eggs white until foamy, gradually add bran a tablespoon at a time. Beat until stiff, but not dry. Spoon over each custard. Chill thoroughly before serving. Serves 4.

EGGFUL HALF MOONS

6 eggs
¼ cup grated cheese

¼ cup grated carrots
¼ cup finely chopped pimiento
¼ cup finely chopped green pepper
¼ cup bran

Beat eggs until thick and lemon colored. Heat a lightly oiled griddle until a drop of water sizzles on top. Pour eggs onto griddle in 4 equal amounts. Sprinkle with cheese, carrots, pimiento, green pepper and bran. When omelet is set, fold in half to form a half-moon shape. Serve immediately. Serves 4.

FLUFFY EGG NESTS

4 slices hot, buttered whole-grain toast
4 egg whites
4 egg yolks
½ to 1 cup grated cheese
¼ cup bran

Place hot buttered toast on cookie sheet. Beat egg whites until stiff, but not dry. Pile whites on toast, making an indentation in the center of each. Carefully slip an egg yolk into each indentation. Sprinkle with grated cheese and bran. Bake in a moderate (350°F.) oven for 15 minutes or until whites are lightly browned and yolks are set. Serves 4.

FRUIT OMELET

3 eggs
3 tablespoons water
1 tablespoon butter
½ cup fresh pineapple chunks or ½ cup fresh strawberries, sliced
2 tablespoons bran

Mix eggs and water with fork. Heat butter in skillet just hot enough to sizzle a drop of water. Pour in egg mixture.

Mixture should set at edges at once. As the mixture thickens, carefully draw these portions with a spatula or fork toward the center so that the uncooked portions flow to the bottom. Tilt skillet as it is necessary to hasten flow of uncooked eggs. Keep mixture as level as possible. When eggs are set and surface is still moist, increase heat to brown bottom quickly. To serve, put ½ cup desired fruit in center of omelet and fold in half. Sprinkle top with bran. Serves 1 or 2.

FRENCH TOAST

4 eggs, beaten
⅔ cup milk
¼ cup bran
12 slices whole-grain bread
2 tablespoons oil

Combine eggs, milk, and bran. Dip each side of bread in egg mixture. Brown on both sides in oil on a hot griddle—3 to 4 minutes on each side. Serve promptly. Serves 6. (TIP: Add ½ teaspoon cinnamon to egg mixture before dipping bread.)

POACHED EGGS SUPREME

1 10½-oz. condensed Cheddar cheese soup
2 tablespoons chopped green pepper
¼ cup Cheddar cheese
6 slices whole-grain toast
6 eggs
¼ cup bran

Combine soup and green pepper. Spread cheese on toast. Poach eggs until firm. Place eggs on toast. Cover with bran and hot soup mixture. Serve immediately. Serves 6.

DEVILED EGGS

6 eggs
¼ cup mayonnaise or salad dressing
¼ cup bran
Paprika

Hard-cook eggs. Cool eggs under cold running water 5 to 10 minutes. Peel shells from eggs. Cut eggs in half lengthwise. Mash yolks with mayonnaise and bran until smooth. Fill whites with this smooth mixture. Sprinkle with paprika. Serves 6.

BRAN 'N' SPROUT OMELET

1 tablespoon vegetable oil
1 cup bean sprouts
½ cup bran
2 eggs
2 tablespoons milk

Heat oil in warm skillet. Stir in sprouts and bran. Cook gently until sprouts are limp. Put in side dish. Now break eggs in a bowl. Fork-beat until yolks and whites are combined. Add milk. Heat 1 teaspoon of oil in a skillet. Pour in egg mixture. As egg cooks on bottom and sides, stab with fork so that the soft egg on top goes to the bottom of the pan. Spread slightly cooked sprouts and bran over egg. Fold in half, brown in a hot oven for 3 minutes. Serves 2.

BAKED FLUFFY "BRANLET"

6 eggs, separated
3 tablespoons fruit juice
1 tablespoon bran
¼ tablespoon chervil
2 tablespoons oil

Beat eggs yolks until golden yellow. Now blend together all ingredients, except egg whites. Beat egg whites stiff and fold into mixture. Preheat oiled skillet, turn mixture into it, and bake at 300°F. for 15 to 20 minutes. Serves 6.

EGGS FOO YOUNG

5 eggs
½ cup water
¼ cup slivered onions
½ cup bean sprouts or finely cut celery
¼ cup bran
½ cup chopped cooked lean meat, chicken,
    or turkey
½ cup sliced water chestnuts or mushrooms
Soy sauce

Beat together eggs and water. Add all remaining ingredients. Spread in a thin layer in a well-oiled skillet. Brown on both sides. Flavor with soy sauce, according to taste. Serves 4.

EGG TIMBALES

1 tablespoon butter
1 tablespoon whole-grain flour
2 tablespoons bran
⅔ cup milk
3 egg yolks, beaten until thick
1 tablespoon chopped parsley
3 egg whites, beaten until stiff

Melt butter. Blend in flour and bran. Add milk slowly. Stir together until thick and smooth. Remove from heat. Stir in all remaining ingredients except egg whites. When thoroughly combined, cut and fold in egg whites. Turn into oiled custard cups. Set in pan of hot water. Bake at 350°F. until firm (35 minutes). Unmold. Serves 4.

EGG CROQUETTES

1 10½-oz. can condensed cream of celery, chicken,
   or mushroom soup
8 hard-cooked eggs, sieved or very finely chopped
¼ cup bran
2 tablespoons minced parsley
2 tablespoons minced onion
2 tablespoons shortening
⅓ cup milk

Mix ¼ cup soup with eggs, bran, parsley, and onion;
form into 6 croquettes. If mixture is difficult to handle,
chill before shaping. Roll in additional bran. Sauté croquettes slowly in shortening until browned. Meanwhile,
combine remaining soup with milk. Heat. Serve as sauce
over croquettes. Serves 3.

QUICK EGG CURRY

1 10½-oz. can condensed cream of mushroom soup
⅓ cup milk
1 teaspoon curry powder
4 hard-cooked eggs, sliced
4 slices whole-grain bread, toasted
¼ cup bran

Stir soup until smooth. Blend in milk and curry powder.
Heat, stirring often. Add eggs. Serve over toast with bran.
Also try shredded coconut, toasted slivered almonds, sun-
dried raisins. Serves 4.

EGGS IN CHEESE SAUCE

1 10½-oz. can condensed cream of vegetable,
    celery, or mushroom soup
⅓ to ½ cup milk
½ cup shredded Cheddar cheese
¼ cup bran
4 hard-cooked eggs, sliced
4 slices whole-grain toast
2 sprigs parsley, minced

Combine soup, milk, cheese, and bran. Cook over low heat until cheese melts. Stir often. Add eggs. Serve on toast. Garnish with parsley. Serves 4.

CHAPTER 19

BRAN RECIPES FOR ALLERGICS

RYE BISCUITS
(Without eggs or wheat)

1⅓ cups rye flour
½ cup soybean flour
1 tablespoon baking powder
2 tablespoons bran
1 tablespoon honey
¼ cup vegetable oil
¾ cup milk

Preheat oven to very hot (450°F.). Mix dry ingredients thoroughly. Add honey. Mix in oil only until mixture is crumbly. Add milk gradually and stir until a soft dough is formed. Place on floured surface and roll or pat to a thickness of about ½ inch. Cut into 2-inch rounds. Place on ungreased baking sheet. Bake 12 minutes or until very lightly browned. Makes 1 dozen 2-inch biscuits.

CORN MEAL MUFFINS
(Without eggs, milk or wheat)

1 cup undegerminated corn meal
½ cup rye flour
⅓ cup rice flour
1 tablespoon bran
2 tablespoons baking powder
¼ cup honey
1 cup water
¼ cup vegetable oil

Preheat oven to moderate (375°F.). Oil muffin tins. Mix dry ingredients thoroughly. Add honey, water, and oil. Mix well. Fill muffin tins about half full. Bake 30 minutes or until very lightly browned and firm to touch. Makes 12 small muffins.

ORANGE-NUT BREAD
(Without eggs, milk or wheat)

2¼ cups rolled oats, ground
4 teaspoons baking powder
¼ teaspoon baking soda
½ cup honey
¾ cup chopped nuts
2 tablespoons oil
¾ cup orange juice
1 tablespoon orange rind, grated

Preheat oven to moderate (350°F.). Oil 9 x 5-inch loaf pan. Mix dry ingredients thoroughly. Add honey, nuts, oil, orange juice, and rind. Stir until dry ingredients are well moistened. Pour into pan. Bake 60 minutes or until firm to touch. To prevent the top of loaf from cracking, cover with aluminum foil during the first 20 minutes of baking. NOTE: Grind rolled oats in a food chopper, using the fine cutting blade. Makes 1 loaf; 16 slices, ½-inch thick.

SPOONBREAD
(Without wheat)

3 cups milk
1 cup undegerminated corn meal
2 tablespoons butter or margarine
4 eggs, separated

Preheat oven to hot (400°F.). Oil 1½-quart casserole. Combine milk, corn meal. Cook over low heat, stirring constantly, until thickened. Add butter. Cool the mixture. Stir in beaten egg yolks. Beat egg whites until stiff, but not dry. Fold into corn meal mixture. Pour into casserole. Bake 35 or 40 minutes, or until set. Serve hot. Serves 6.

ROLLED OAT MUFFINS
(Without eggs, milk, or wheat)

1 cup rolled oats, ground
¾ cup rice flour
2 tablespoons baking powder
1 teaspoon cinnamon
¼ cup honey
½ cup raisins
1¼ cups water
¼ cup oil

Preheat oven to hot (425°F.). Oil muffin tins. Mix dry ingredients thoroughly. Add honey, raisins, water, and oil. Mix well. Fill muffin tins about two-thirds full. Bake 20 minutes or until lightly browned. NOTE: Grind rolled oats in a food chopper, using the fine cutting blade. Makes 12 medium-sized muffins.

RYE CRACKERS
(Without eggs or wheat)

1¾ cups rye flour
1 cup rice flour
2 tablespoons bran
1 teaspoon baking soda
½ cup oil
1 cup buttermilk

Preheat oven to moderate (375°F.). Mix dry ingredients thoroughly. Mix in oil only until mixture is crumbly. Add buttermilk and mix well. Place dough on a well-floured surface. Roll very thin. Cut into strips 3 x 1½ inches. Place with sides touching on baking sheet. Bake 18 minutes or until lightly browned. NOTE: Sprinkle tops of crackers with more bran, before baking, if desired. Makes 75 crackers, 3 x 1½ inches.

RYE MUFFINS
(Without eggs, milk, or wheat)

1¼ cups rye flour
½ cup rice flour
4 teaspoons baking powder
¼ cup honey
1 cup water
¼ cup oil

Preheat oven to moderate (375°F.). Mix dry ingredients thoroughly. Add honey, water, and oil and mix well. Fill oiled muffin tins about half full. Bake 25 minutes or until lightly browned. Makes 12 small muffins.

WAFFLES
(Without wheat)

1½ cups rice flour
1 tablespoon baking powder
1 teaspoon bran
¼ cup honey
1½ cups milk
2 egg yolks, beaten
3 tablespoons oil
2 egg whites, stiffly beaten

Mix dry ingredients well. Add honey. Beat in milk, egg yolks, and oil. Fold in egg whites. Bake in hot waffle iron. Makes 16 waffles, 7 inches in diameter.

FIG-NUT PUDDING
(Without milk or wheat)

2 eggs
½ cup honey
3 tablespoons rice flour
1 teaspoon baking powder
½ teaspoon cinnamon
1 cup dried figs, chopped
1 cup chopped nuts

Preheat oven to low (300°F.). Oil an 8 x 8 x 2-inch baking pan. Beat eggs until thick and light in color. Add honey to eggs gradually, beating constantly. Mix dry ingredients. Stir into egg mixture. Add figs and nuts. Beat thoroughly. Pour into baking pan. Bake 40 minutes or until mixture is firm to touch. Serves 6, ½ cup each.

DATE CAKE
(Without milk or wheat)

1 cup boiling water
1 cup chopped dates
½ cup oil
½ cup honey
1 egg
1 teaspoon vanilla
1½ cups rice flour
¾ cup soybean flour
2 tablespoons bran
4 teaspoons baking powder
¼ teaspoon nutmeg

Preheat oven to moderate (350°F.). Oil an 8 x 8 x 2-inch baking pan. Pour boiling water over dates. Cool to lukewarm. Beat oil and honey until very creamy and fluffy. Add egg and vanilla and beat well. Mix dry ingredients thoroughly. Add alternately with dates to the creamy mixture. Beat well after each addition. Pour into baking pan. Bake 50 minutes or until cake begins to leave sides of pan. Cake may be served warm or cold.

NOTE: Top the cooled cake with a creamy frosting. Make frosting by blending together 1 cup honey, 3 tablespoons oil, ½ teaspoon flavoring and enough water or fruit juice for a good spreading consistency. Makes 9 servings, 2½ x 2½ inches.

CHIFFON CAKE
(Without milk or wheat)

¾ cup rice flour
1 tablespoon bran
1½ teaspoons baking powder
½ cup honey
¼ cup oil
3 egg yolks, beaten
¼ cup water
1 tablespoon lemon juice
1 teaspoon grated lemon rind
3 egg whites
¼ teaspoon cream of tartar

Preheat oven to moderate (350°F.). Mix dry ingredients thoroughly. Add honey, oil, egg yolks, water, lemon juice, and rind. Beat until very smooth. Beat egg whites until stiff, but not dry. Fold into egg yolk mixture. Pour into ungreased 8 x 8 x 2-inch baking pan. Bake 35 minutes or until firm to touch. Invert in pan on rack to cool. Makes 9 servings, 2½ x 2½ inches.

PINEAPPLE UPSIDE-DOWN CAKE
(Without eggs, milk, or wheat)

¼ cup oil
¼ cup honey
6 slices canned pineapple, drained

⅓ cup shortening
⅓ cup honey
1 cup rye flour
¾ cup rice flour
1 tablespoon bran
4 teaspoons baking powder
1 cup pineapple juice

Preheat oven to moderate (375°F.). Combine ¼ cup oil with ¼ cup honey in an 8 x 8 x 2-inch baking pan in the oven. Place pineapple slices in this oil-honey mixture. Beat ⅓ cup shortening with ⅓ cup honey until very creamy and fluffy. Mix dry ingredients thoroughly. Add alternately with pineapple juice to the creamy mixture. Beat well after each addition. Pour batter over pineapple. Bake 45 minutes or until cake begins to leave sides of pan. Invert in pan on plate. Cake will ease out of pan in a few minutes. Serve while still warm. Makes 9 servings, 2½ x 2½ inches.

SPICE CAKE
(Without eggs, milk, or wheat)

1¼ cups boiling water
1 cup raisins
⅓ cup vegetable shortening
⅔ cup honey
1 teaspoon vanilla
1 cup rye flour
1 tablespoon bran
1 teaspoon cinnamon
4 teaspoons baking powder
1 cup undegerminated corn meal

Preheat oven to low (325°F.). Oil an 8 x 8 x 2-inch baking pan. Pour boiling water over raisins. Cool to luke-warm. Beat shortening, honey, and vanilla until very creamy and fluffy. Mix dry ingredients thoroughly. Add alternately with raisins to the creamy mixture. Beat well after each addition. Pour into baking pan. Bake 45 minutes or until cake begins to leave sides of pan. Serve warm, if desired. Makes 9 servings, 2½ x 2½ inches.

FIG BARS
(Without milk or wheat)

1 cup dried figs, chopped
1 cup nuts, chopped
⅔ cup honey
2 eggs, beaten
¼ cup rice flour
1 tablespoon oil
1 tablespoon lemon juice
1 tablespoon bran

Preheat oven to slow (325°F.) Oil an 8 x 8 x 2-inch baking pan. Mix figs, nuts, honey, and eggs thoroughly. Stir flour into fig mixture. Add oil and lemon juice. Beat well. Add bran. Mix. Spread mixture in baking pan. Bake 40 minutes or until lightly browned. Cool. Cut into bars ¾ by 2 inches. Makes 40 bars.

OATMEAL LACE COOKIES
(Without eggs, milk, or wheat)

1 cup vegetable shortening
⅔ cup honey
1 teaspoon vanilla
1 cup rice flour
1 teaspoon bran
4 teaspoons baking powder
¾ cup water
3 cups rolled oats
½ cup chopped nuts

Beat shortening, honey, and vanilla until fluffy. Mix flour, bran, and baking powder thoroughly. Add alternately with water to the creamy mixture. Add rolled oats and nuts;

mix well. Chill overnight. Next day, preheat oven to moderate (350°F.). Lightly oil baking sheets. Drop batter by teaspoonfuls onto baking sheets. Bake 10 minutes or until lightly browned. Makes 5 dozen medium-sized cookies.

MOLASSES DROP COOKIES
(Without eggs, milk, or wheat)

½ cup vegetable oil
⅓ cup honey
½ cup molasses
1¾ cups rye flour
1 teaspoon ginger
1 teaspoon cinnamon
¼ teaspoon ground cloves
1 tablespoon bran
1½ teaspoons baking powder
¼ teaspoon baking soda
⅓ cup water
½ teaspoon vinegar

Beat oil with honey until very creamy and fluffy. Beat molasses into the creamy mixture. Mix dry ingredients thoroughly. Add alternately with combined water and vinegar to the creamy mixture. Beat well after each addition. Chill thoroughly. Preheat oven to moderate (350°F.). Lightly oil baking sheets. Drop batter by teaspoonfuls onto baking sheets. Bake 8 to 10 minutes or until lightly browned and set. Makes 4 dozen small cookies.

PIE CRUST
(Without eggs or wheat)

1 tablespoon undegerminated corn meal
1 cup bran
¼ cup honey
⅓ cup butter or margarine, melted

Preheat oven to moderate (375°F.). Mix dry ingredients with honey thoroughly. Press into 9-inch pie pan covered with butter. Bake 5 to 8 minutes. NOTE: Cool, then fill with favorite pie filling. Makes one 9-inch pie shell.

CHAPTER 20

DESSERTS

DELUXE DATE COFFEE CAKE

⅓ cup honey
1 tablespoon whole-wheat flour
1 tablespoon cinnamon
¼ cup chopped nuts
¼ cup finely cut, pitted dates
¼ cup regular margarine or butter, melted
1¼ cups sifted all-purpose unbleached flour
1½ teaspoons baking powder
½ cup bran
½ cup soft shortening
⅓ cup honey
1 egg
½ cup milk
½ teaspoon vanilla flavoring

Place honey, 1 tablespoon flour, cinnamon, nuts, and dates in small mixing bowl; mix well. Add margarine, stirring until mixture is crumbly. Set aside for topping. Now sift together the 1¼ cups flour, baking powder; stir in bran. Set aside. Next, measure shortening and honey into large mixing bowl; beat until light and fluffy. Add egg, milk and vanilla; beat well. Add sifted dry ingredients, mixing *only until combined*. Spread batter evenly in oiled 8 x 8 x 2-inch baking pan. Sprinkle date topping evenly over batter. Bake in moderate oven (350°F.) about 45 minutes or until wooden pick inserted near center comes out clean. Cut into squares; serve warm or at room temperature. Serves 9.

FRUIT COCKTAIL COBBLER

⅓ cup honey
3 tablespoons arrowroot powder
2 17-oz. cans (3½ cups) fruit cocktail,
    undrained
½ teaspoon grated orange peel
1 cup sifted all-purpose unbleached flour
2 teaspoons baking powder
¼ cup honey
¼ cup soft shortening
1 egg
⅓ cup milk
½ cup bran

Combine honey and arrowroot powder in large saucepan; stir in fruit cocktail and orange peel. Cook over medium heat until mixture begins to bubble, stirring constantly. Continue cooking 2 minutes, stirring occasionally. Spread evenly in ungreased 9 x 9 x 2-inch baking pan. Set aside. Sift together flour and baking powder; add honey. Place in large mixing bowl. Cut in shortening until mixture resembles coarse cornmeal. Set aside. In a small mixing bowl, beat egg until foamy. Add milk and bran; stir to combine. Let stand 1 to 2 minutes or until most of liquid is absorbed. Add cereal mixture to flour/shortening mixture, stirring *only until combined*. Drop by spoonfuls, one for each serving, over fruit cocktail mixture. Bake in moderately hot oven (400°F.) about 25 minutes or until cake topping is lightly browned. Spoon into dessert dishes and serve warm with whipped topping or half-and-half. Serves 9.

CHOCOLATE SNOW DROPS

1 cup sifted all-purpose unbleached flour
1 teaspoon baking powder
¼ teaspoon baking soda
½ cup coarsely chopped nuts

⅓ cup regular margarine or butter, softened
⅔ cup honey
1 egg
2 squares (2 ounces or 4 tablespoons) unsweetened chocolate, melted (or use carob powder as nonchocolate substitute)
½ cup bran
½ cup buttermilk or sour milk
½ teaspoon vanilla flavoring

Sift together flour, baking powder, soda; stir in nuts. Set aside. Measure margarine and honey into large mixing bowl; beat well. Add egg and melted chocolate (or carob); mix thoroughly. Mix in bran cereal, buttermilk, and vanilla. Add sifted dry ingredients; mix until combined. Drop by tablespoons onto lightly oiled baking sheets. Bake in moderate oven (375°F.) about 12 minutes or until cooky springs back when lightly touched. Remove immediately from baking sheets; cool on wire racks. Makes about 3½ dozen cookies, 2¼ inches in diameter.

VARIATION: Press walnut half gently into top of each cooky just before baking.

KWIK KRAZY KAKE

1½ cups sifted all-purpose unbleached flour
1 teaspoon baking soda
1 teaspoon cinnamon
¼ cup cocoa or carob powder
½ cup bran
1 cup cold strong coffee or Postum
1 cup honey
¼ cup vegetable oil
1 tablespoon vinegar
1 teaspoon vanilla flavoring

Sift together flour, soda, cinnamon, and cocoa or carob powder. Set aside. Now measure bran and coffee or Postum into ungreased 8 x 8 x 2-inch baking pan; stir to combine. Let stand 1 to 2 minutes or until most of liquid is absorbed. Mix in honey, oil, vinegar, and vanilla. Add sifted dry ingredients; stir until smooth. Bake in moderate oven (350°F.) about 40 minutes or until wooden pick inserted near center comes out clean. Cool completely on wire rack. Cut into squares. Serve with orange sauce, lemon sauce, or cinnamon-flavored whipped topping. Sprinkle with chopped nuts if desired. Serves 9.

LUSCIOUS APRICOT BARS

⅔ cup finely cut sun-dried apricots
Hot water
½ cup margarine or butter
⅓ cup honey
1 cup sifted all-purpose unbleached flour
½ cup bran
½ teaspoon baking powder
1 cup honey
2 eggs
½ teaspoon vanilla flavoring
½ cup finely chopped nuts

Rinse apricots; place in small mixing bowl. Cover with very hot water. Let stand 10 minutes or until fruit is tender; drain well. Set aside. For crust, measure margarine, honey, and ½ cup of the flour into small mixing bowl; beat until smooth and creamy. Mix in bran. Spread mixture evenly in bottom of ungreased 8 x 8 x 2-inch baking pan. Bake in moderate oven (350°F.) about 25 minutes or until lightly browned. Remove from oven; cool slightly. While crust is baking, sift together the remaining ½ cup flour and baking powder. Set aside. Now place honey and eggs in large mixing bowl; beat well. Add sifted dry ingredients, vanilla, nuts, and apricots; mix well. Spread mixture over baked crust. Return to moderate oven (350°F.); bake 50 minutes or until lightly browned. Cool; cut into bars. Makes 32 bars, 2 inches x 1 inch.

VARIATION: Substitute ¾ cup finely cut pitted prunes for dried apricots.

DOTTED PUMPKIN CAKE

2 cups sifted all-purpose unbleached flour
2 teaspoons baking powder
1 teaspoon baking soda
1½ teaspoons cinnamon
½ teaspoon ground cloves
¼ teaspoon allspice
¼ teaspoon ginger
1½ cups honey
4 eggs
1 1-lb can (2 cups) pumpkin
1 cup vegetable oil
1 cup bran
1 cup carob (or semisweet chocolate morsels)
1 cup coarsely chopped pecans

Sift together flour, baking powder, soda, and spices. Add honey. Set aside. In large mixing bowl, beat eggs until foamy. Add pumpkin, vegetable oil, and bran and mix well. Add sifted dry ingredients mixing *only until combined*. Stir in carob or chocolate morsels and pecans. Spread evenly in ungreased 10 x 4-inch tube pan. Bake in moderate oven (350°F.) about 1 hour and 10 minutes or until wooden pick inserted near center comes out clean. Invert and cool completely before removing from pan. Serves 16.

BAKED BUCKWHEAT PUDDING

2 eggs, beaten
½ cup buckwheat groats (kasha)
1½ quarts milk
¾ cup molasses
1½ teaspoons ginger
3 tablespoons honey

Combine eggs and groats. In medium-sized skillet, scald 2 cups of milk. Stir in groats. Cook, tightly covered, over low heat, 10 minutes, stirring occasionally. Blend in 2 more cups milk, molasses, ginger, and honey. Pour into 1½-quart baking dish. Bake, uncovered, in moderate oven (325°F.) 1 hour. Stir in remaining 2 cups milk; continue baking 1¼ hours longer. Serve warm. Serves 6.

FRUIT AND NUT RING

    1 egg, beaten
    1 cup buckwheat groats (kasha)
    3 cups water
    2 eggs, beaten
    ¼ cup honey
    ½ cup chopped pecans
    ½ cup seedless raisins
    ½ cup chopped dates
    1 teaspoon cinnamon

In medium-sized saucepan, combine 1 egg, beaten; then add groats. Stir in water; bring to boil. Cook over low heat 10 minutes, stirring occasionally. Combine remaining ingredients; stir into groat mixture. Oil a 1-quart ring mold; dust with dry groats. Pack hot groat mixture into mold. Bake in moderate oven (350°F.) 30 minutes. Remove from oven; let stand 10 minutes. Unmold on serving platter. Serve warm with lemon sauce, if desired. Serves 6 to 8.

PRUNE-APPLE PUDDING

    1 egg, beaten
    ½ cup buckwheat groats (kasha)
    2 tablespoons shortening
    1 cup water
    2 eggs, separated
    ¼ cup honey
    1 cup chopped, peeled tart apple

1 cup chopped cooked prunes
1 teaspoon grated lemon rind
1 tablespoon lemon juice

Combine beaten egg, groats. In medium-sized pan, cook groat mixture in shortening 3 minutes or until lightly toasted, stirring often. Stir in water; bring to boil. Cook tightly covered over low heat for 10 minutes. Remove from heat; cook, uncovered, about 15 minutes. Beat egg yolks, blending in honey; add fruit, lemon rind, and juice. Stir into groat mixture. Beat egg whites until stiff, but not dry. Carefully fold into groat-fruit mixture. Turn into oiled 1½-quart baking dish. Bake in moderate oven (350°F.) 45 minutes, or until firm. Serve warm with custard, lemon, or orange sauce if desired. Serves 4 to 6.

CHAPTER 21

CONFECTIONS, COOKIES, SNACKS

BRAN-DATE DAINTIES

¾ cup honey
1 cup finely cut, pitted dates
2 eggs
1 teaspoon vanilla flavoring
2 cups bran
Flaked coconut

Combine honey, dates, and eggs in cold skillet. Cook about 10 minutes over medium heat, stirring constantly, or until mixture starts to thicken. Remove from heat. Now stir in vanilla and bran; mix well. Dip measuring teaspoon in ice water, then drop rounded teaspoonfuls of mixture onto waxed paper or buttered baking sheets. Roll in flaked coconut, if desired. Chill before serving. Makes 35 dainties.

OATMEAL PIE

2 eggs
¼ cup honey
¾ cup dark corn syrup
2 tablespoons all-purpose unbleached flour
¼ cup butter or margarine, melted
1 teaspoon vanilla
¾ cup oats, uncooked
⅓ cup flaked or shredded coconut
One 9-inch unbaked pie shell

Beat eggs until foamy. Gradually add honey; beat until thick. Stir in remaining ingredients; blend well. Pour into pie shell. Bake in preheated moderate oven (350°F.) about 45 minutes or until center of pie is firm. Cool. Serve with yoghurt, if desired. Makes one 9-inch pie.

DATE RING

½ cup shortening, soft
½ cup honey
2 eggs
1 teaspoon vanilla
1½ cups sifted all-purpose unbleached flour
1½ teaspoons baking powder
½ teaspoon baking soda
½ teaspoon cinnamon
¼ teaspoon cloves
1¼ cups buttermilk
½ cup chopped nutmeats
1½ cups chopped pitted dates
1 cup uncooked oats

Beat shortening and honey together until creamy. Add eggs, one at a time, beating well after each addition. Blend in vanilla. Sift together flour, baking powder, soda, and spices. Add to creamed mixture alternately with buttermilk; blend well. Stir in nutmeats, dates, oats. Pour into well-oiled and floured 1½-quart ring mold. Bake in preheated slow oven (325°F.) 45 to 50 minutes. Loosen edges; cool on wire rack about 15 minutes. Remove from mold. Cool. Makes one cake ring.

SPICY APPLE CRISP

4 cups peeled and sliced cooking apples
1 tablespoon lemon juice
1/3 cup sifted all-purpose unbleached flour
1 cup oats, uncooked
1/2 cup honey
1 teaspoon cinnamon
1/3 butter or margarine, melted

Place apples in a shallow baking dish. Sprinkle with lemon juice. Combine flour, oats, honey, cinnamon, and butter, mixing until crumbly. Sprinkle crumb mixture over apples. Bake in preheated moderate oven (375°F.) about 30 minutes or until apples are tender. Serve warm or cold. Serves 6.

SPICY PEACH CRISP: Use 4 cups peeled and sliced fresh peaches in place of apples in preceding recipe. If peaches are tart, sprinkle with honey to sweeten. Prepare and bake as directed above.

BRAN-COCONUT PUDDING

3 tablespoons arrowroot powder
1/4 cup honey
2 cups milk
2 egg yolks, beaten
2 tablespoons butter or margarine
1 teaspoon vanilla
1/2 cup shredded or flaked coconut
1/2 cup bran

Mix arrowroot powder and honey in a heavy saucepan. Gradually add milk to blend. Stir over moderate heat about 7 minutes or until mixture thickens. Stir a little of the hot mixture into egg yolks; then stir yolks into remaining hot mixture. Cook 1 minute longer, stirring constantly. Mix in butter, vanilla, coconut, and bran. Serve warm or chilled. NOTE: For this recipe, use only clean eggs with no cracks in shells. Serves 6.

PECAN CHESS PIE

⅔ cup honey
½ cup bran
1 tablespoon all-purpose unbleached flour
2 eggs
¼ cup milk
½ cup butter or margarine, melted
1 teaspoon vanilla
¾ cup or 1 cup (as desired) pecans, chopped
One 9-inch pastry shell, unbaked

Preheat oven to moderate (375°F.). Mix honey with bran and flour. Beat in eggs and milk. Stir in melted butter, vanilla, and nuts. Pour mixture into pastry shell. Bake 40 minutes or until knife inserted in the center comes out clean. Cool before serving. Makes one 9-inch pie, about 8 servings.

PEANUT BUTTER COOKIES

1 cup vegetable shortening
1 cup bran
¾ cup honey
2 eggs
1 teaspoon vanilla
2½ cups all-purpose unbleached flour
¾ teaspoon baking soda
½ teaspoon baking powder

Preheat oven to moderate (375°F.). Beat shortening and peanut butter together until creamy. Add bran, beating thoroughly. Beat in eggs and vanilla. Mix remaining ingredients and stir into peanut butter mixture. Shape dough into 1-inch balls. Place about 2 inches apart on an ungreased baking sheet. Flatten each by pressing criss-cross with a fork. Bake 10 to 15 minutes until lightly browned. Remove from baking dish while warm. Makes 4½ dozen cookies.

NIPPY CHEESE-NUT DIP

2 3-oz. packages softened cream cheese
¼ cup mayonnaise
¼ teaspoon onion powder
Few grains garlic powder
½ cup nuts (pecans, toasted almonds, cashews, or roasted peanuts) finely chopped
2 tablespoons bran

Blend cream cheese with mayonnaise and seasonings. Stir in nuts and bran. Blend thoroughly together. Makes about 1 cup.

SWEET SPICED NUTS

1 tablespoon butter or margarine, melted
1 egg white, slightly beaten
2 cups unroasted almonds, walnuts, and/or pecans
½ cup bran
⅔ cup honey
1½ teaspoons cinnamon
¾ teaspoon allspice

Preheat oven to slow (300°F.). Slowly stir melted butter into beaten egg white. Stir in nuts. Mix in bran, honey, and spices. Spread about one-fourth of the mixture in a 10 x 15-inch shallow baking pan. Coat a few nuts at a time in remaining mixture and arrange in the pan. Sprinkle rest of mixture over nuts. Bake 15 to 20 minutes or until nuts are lightly browned. Remove nuts from oven; stir gently to separate. Cool. Store in tightly closed container. Makes about 4 cups.

COCKTAIL NUTS

2 tablespoons butter or margarine
1 pound mixed nuts with peanuts
1 tablespoon bran
1 teaspoon onion powder
½ teaspoon paprika

Preheat oven to slow (300°F.). Melt butter in a shallow baking pan in the oven. Remove pan from oven and stir in nuts. Sprinkle with bran and seasonings. Bake 15 to 20 minutes or until nuts are heated through, stirring occasionally. Cool. Store in tightly closed container. Makes about 3½ cups.

OLD-FASHIONED RICE PUDDING

½ cup brown rice, uncooked
1½ cups water
⅓ cup honey
½ cup seedless raisins
2 tablespoons bran
2 cups half-and-half (milk and cream)
1 teaspoon vanilla

Place rice and water in heavy 2-quart saucepan; cover tightly. Boil gently, stirring occasionally until rice is tender and most of water is absorbed, about 15 minutes. Stir in honey, raisins, bran, and half-and-half. Cook over very low heat, stirring occasionally, until pudding has a creamy consistency. (Pudding thickens some on cooling.) Do not allow pudding to boil. Stir in vanilla. Serve warm or cold. Serves 6.

BRAN MACAROONS

2 egg whites
⅔ cup honey
¼ teaspoon almond extract
1 cup shredded coconut
1½ cups bran

Preheat oven to moderate (350°F.). Grease baking sheet. Beat egg whites until foamy; add honey gradually, while beating constantly until stiff peaks form. Beat in flavoring. Fold in coconut and bran gently. Drop by teaspoonfuls onto baking sheet, about 2 inches apart. Bake 15 to 20 minutes or until lightly browned. NOTE: Remove macaroons immediately. To remove them easily, place baking sheet on a damp cloth; use a spatula or pancake turner. Makes about 3 dozen cookies.

OAT-BRAN BONBONS

1 cup butter or margarine, softened
⅔ cup honey
2 teaspoons vanilla
1¾ cups all-purpose unbleached flour
1 cup rolled oats, uncooked
½ cup bran

FROSTING:

1 cup honey
1 teaspoon lemon juice
1 teaspoon vanilla
4 teaspoons water
1 tablespoon very dark fruit juice (prune or cranberry for instance) for coloring

Preheat oven to moderate (350°F.). Beat butter until creamy. Add honey and beat until fluffy. Blend in vanilla. Mix flour with butter mixture until blended. Stir in rolled oats and bran. Shape dough into balls about 1 inch in diameter; place about 2 inches apart on ungreased baking sheet. Bake 25 to 30 minutes. Cookies will be brown on bottom but not on top. Remove from cookie sheet. Cool. Now, blend all frosting ingredients together. Spread on cooled cookies. Makes 4 to 5 dozen cookies.

CRUNCHY DESSERT TOPPING

2 cups rolled oats
¼ cup bran
⅓ cup honey
⅓ cup butter or margarine, melted
½ cup nuts, chopped

Preheat oven to moderate (350°F.). Combine ingredients and mix until crumbly. Spread mixture loosely in a 12 x 18-inch baking pan. Bake, stirring occasionally, until lightly browned, about 10 minutes. Let cool 15 minutes; then stir lightly with a fork. Store in a tightly covered container in the refrigerator. NOTE: Serve on ice cream, fruit or chilled pudding. Makes about 4 cups.

APPENDIX

WEIGHTS AND MEASURES

Because we will soon be transforming to the metric system, you may be needing to refer to these lists and charts:

WEIGHTS

10 Milligrams	= 1 Centigram
10 Centigrams	= 1 Decigram
10 Decigrams	= 1 Gram
10 Grams	= 1 Decagram
10 Decagrams	= 1 Hectogram
10 Hectograms	= 1 Kilogram
100 Kilograms	= 1 Quintal
10 Quintals	= 1 Metric Ton

1 Metric Ton = 2,204.6 Lbs.

SQUARE MEASURE

100 Sq. Millimeters	= 1 Sq. Centimeter
100 Sq. Centimeters	= 1 Sq. Decimeter
100 Sq. Decimeters	= 1 Sq. Meter
100 Sq. Meters	= 1 Sq. Decameter
100 Sq. Decameters	= 1 Sq. Hectometer
100 Sq. Hectometers	= 1 Sq. Kilometer

Sq. Meters x 1.196 = Sq. Yards

CAPACITY MEASURE

10 Milliliters	= 1 Centiliter
10 Centiliters	= 1 Deciliter
10 Deciliters	= 1 Liter
10 Liters	= 1 Decaliter
10 Decaliters	= 1 Hectoliter
10 Hectoliters	= 1 Kiloliter

Gallons x 3.785 = Liters
1 Centiliter = 0.338 Fluid oz.

LINEAR MESURE

10 Millimeters	= 1 Centimeter
10 Centimeters	= 1 Decimeter
10 Decimeters	= 1 Meter
10 Meters	= 1 Decameter
10 Decameters	= 1 Hectometer
10 Hectometers	= 1 Kilometer

Inches x 2.540 = Centimeters

WEIGHTS Metric Equivalent

U.S.A.

		U.S.A.
ounce = 28.35 grams	1 gram = .04 ounce
pound = .45 kilogram	1 kilogram = 2.20 pounds
ton = .91 metric ton	1 metric ton = 1.10 tons

LIQUID MEASURE Metric Equivalent

U.S.A.

	U.S.A.
pint = .47 liter	1 liter = 2.11 pints
quart = .95 liter	1 liter = 1.06 quarts
gallon = 3.79 liters	1 liter = .26 gallons

LENGTH Metric Equivalent

U.S.A.

inch   = 2.54 centimeters
foot   = .30 meter
yard   = .91 meter
mile   = 1.61 kilometers
.39 inch   = 1 centimeter
3.28 feet   = 1 meter
1.09 yards = 1 meter
.62 mile   = 1 kilometer

To convert from kilometers to miles, divide the number of kilometers by 8 and multiply the result by 5.

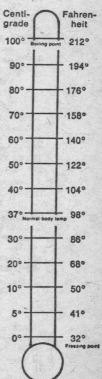

Centigrade		Fahrenheit
100°	Boiling point	212°
90°		194°
80°		176°
70°		158°
60°		140°
50°		122°
40°		104°
37°	Normal body temp	98°
30°		86°
20°		68°
10°		50°
5°		41°
0°	Freezing point	32°

TEMPERATURE

To Compute Fahrenheit: Multiply Centigrade by 1.8 and add 32. Centigrade by 1.8 and add 32.

To Compute Centigrade: Subtract 32 from Fahrenheit and divide by 1.8.